Life in the South During the Civil War

Diane Yancey

San Diego, CA

© 2014 ReferencePoint Press, Inc.
Printed in the United States

For more information, contact:
ReferencePoint Press, Inc.
PO Box 27779
San Diego, CA 92198
www.ReferencePointPress.com

LIBRARY OF CONGRESS CATALOGING-IN-PUBLICATION DATA

Yancey, Diane.
  Life in the South during the Civil War : part of the living history series / by Diane Yancey.
      pages cm. -- (Living history)
  Includes bibliographical references and index.
  ISBN-13: 978-1-60152-578-9 (hardback)
  ISBN-10: 1-60152-578-8 (hardback)
1. Confederate States of America--History--Juvenile literature. 2. Confederate States of America--Politics and government--Juvenile literature. 3. Confederate States of America--Social life and customs--Juvenile literature. 4. United States--History--Civil War, 1861-1865--Juvenile literature. I. Title.
  E487.Y36 2014
  973.7--dc23
                                                                    2013013426

Contents

Foreword

History is a complex and multifaceted discipline that embraces many different areas of human activity. Given the expansive possibilities for the study of history, it is significant that since the advent of formal writing in the Ancient Near East over six thousand years ago, the contents of most nonfiction historical literature have been overwhelmingly limited to politics, religion, warfare, and diplomacy.

Beginning in the 1960s, however, the focus of many historical works experienced a substantive change worldwide. This change resulted from the efforts and influence of an ever-increasing number of progressive contemporary historians who were entering the halls of academia. This new breed of academician, soon accompanied by many popular writers, argued for a major revision of the study of history, one in which the past would be presented from the ground up. What this meant was that the needs, wants, and thinking of ordinary people should and would become an integral part of the human record. As British historian Mary Fulbrook wrote in her 2005 book, *The People's State: East German Society from Hitler to Honecker,* students should be able to view "history with the people put back in." This approach to understanding the lives and times of people of the past has come to be known as social history. According to contemporary social historians, national and international affairs should be viewed not only from the perspective of those empowered to create policy but also through the eyes of those over whom power is exercised.

The American historian and best-selling author, Louis "Studs" Terkel, was one of the pioneers in the field of social history. He is best remembered for his oral histories, which were firsthand accounts of everyday life drawn from the recollections of interviewees who lived during pivotal events or periods in history. Terkel's first book, *Division Street America* (published in 1967), focuses on urban living in and around Chicago and is a compilation of seventy interviews of immigrants and native-born Americans. It was followed by several other oral histories including *Hard Times* (the 1930s depression), *Working* (people's feelings about their jobs), and his 1985 Pulitzer Prize–winning *The Good War* (about life in America before, during, and after World War II).

In keeping with contemporary efforts to present history by people and about people, ReferencePoint's *Living History* series offers students a journey through recorded history as recounted by those who lived it. While modern sources such as those found in *The Good War* and on radio and TV interviews are readily available, those dating to earlier periods in history are scarcer and often more obscure the further back in time one investigates. These important primary sources are there nonetheless waiting to be discovered in literary formats such as posters, letters, and diaries, and in artifacts such as vases, coins, and tombstones. And they are also found in places as varied as ancient Mesopotamia, Charles Dickens's England, and Nazi concentration camps. The *Living History* series uncovers these and other available sources as they relate the "living history" of real people to their student readers.

Important Events

1856

Tension over slavery rises when Congressman Preston Brooks of South Carolina beats Senator Charles Sumner of Massachusetts with a cane on the floor of the US Senate during a debate. Brooks becomes a hero in the South, while Sumner is a martyr in the North.

1860

In November Abraham Lincoln is elected president of the United States; in December South Carolina becomes the first state to secede from the Union.

1862

Union troops capture and occupy New Orleans, Louisiana.

1854　　　1856　　　1858　　　1860　　　1862

1859

In December, abolitionist John Brown is hanged for seizing the federal armory in Harper's Ferry, Virginia, and attempting to spark a slave uprising. Brown becomes a martyr to abolitionists and secession sentiment grows in the South.

1861

Delegates from seceded states meet in Montgomery, Alabama, in February to draw up a constitution and form the Confederate States of America; Jefferson Davis is inaugurated as their president; in April Confederate forces fire on Fort Sumter, South Carolina, marking the beginning of the Civil War; Confederates win the first major battle of the war: the First Battle of Manassas (Bull Run).

of the Civil War

1863
Lincoln issues the Emancipation Proclamation; General Ulysses S. Grant lays siege to the city of Vicksburg, Mississippi, which falls to Union forces in less than two months.

1868
The Fourteenth Amendment to the Constitution is ratified, granting full citizenship to all persons born or naturalized in the United States.

1870
The Fifteenth Amendment is ratified, prohibiting any state from denying the right to vote because of race, color, or previous condition of servitude.

| 1864 | 1866 | 1868 | 1870 | 1872 |

1867
The First Reconstruction Act, passed by Congress, temporarily places the South under military rule and requires that new state constitutions give blacks the vote as a condition for readmittance to the Union.

1865
Columbia, South Carolina, falls to Sherman's troops and is burned; the Confederate government flees when Union troops occupy Richmond, Virginia; in April Confederate general Robert E. Lee surrenders to Grant at Appomattox Court House in Virginia; Jefferson Davis and his family are captured outside of Irwinville, Georgia; in June the Civil War officially ends when General Edmund Kirby Smith, commander of Confederate forces west of the Mississippi, signs the surrender.

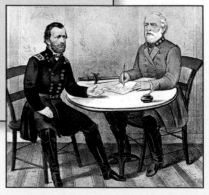

1864
Union forces lay siege to the city of Petersburg, Virginia; Union troops under William Tecumseh Sherman capture the city of Atlanta, Georgia.

A Terrible Thing

Life in the South during the Civil War was a time of almost universal suffering and sacrifice. After the South seceded, the North unleashed its full might upon the rebels—targeting both soldiers and civilians—in a determined effort to bring the newly formed Confederate states back into the federal Union. Union general William Tecumseh Sherman described such warfare: "We are not only fighting hostile armies, but a hostile people, and must make old and young, rich and poor feel the hard hand of war."[1]

To achieve their ends, between 1861 and 1865 Union troops burned and destroyed cities, plantations, crops, animals, warehouses, and railroads. They caused millions of dollars of damage and turned civilians into refugees. Swaths of destruction were cut through Georgia, South Carolina, and North Carolina. The fertile Shenandoah Valley in western Virginia was ransacked and burned. Alabama-born major Henry Hitchcock, who served on Sherman's staff, declared that "it is a terrible thing to consume and destroy the sustenance [support] of thousands of people, [but if the strategy serves] to paralyze their husbands and fathers who are fighting . . . it is mercy in the end."[2]

Principles to Die For

Unaware of what they would be called on to endure, most white Southerners felt that going to war was unavoidable. In the decades before the conflict, they were increasingly unhappy with the Northern states and the federal government. The North had become a fast-paced, forward-thinking, industrialized society that had abolished slavery. The South was largely rural and agrarian, dependent on millions of slaves to grow and harvest crops such as cotton, sugar, and tobacco that were virtually the sole support of the economy.

By the late 1850s, due to the activism of Northerners who wanted to abolish slavery, Southerners were panicking over the thought that they were going to lose the right to own slaves. They began to talk of secession, severing ties with the United States. Most were convinced that they had the right to leave the Union if they so desired. With the 1860 election of Abraham Lincoln (derisively known to some as a Black Republican because of his views on slavery), they also became convinced that the federal government was going to abolish slavery immediately and ruin their way of life. Thus, they decided to act.

On December 20, 1860, South Carolina became the first state to leave the Union. It was followed in 1861 by Mississippi, Florida, Alabama, Georgia, Louisiana, Texas, Arkansas, Tennessee, North Carolina, and Virginia. These states quickly joined together to become the Confederate States of America in order to have as much strength as possible to fight against the powerful Union. The Confederacy's vice president, Alexander H. Stephens, declared:

> The idea has been given out at the North, and even in the border States, that we are too small and too weak to maintain a separate nationality. This is a great mistake. . . . With such an area of territory as we have—with such an amount of population—with a climate and soil unsurpassed by any on the face of the earth— with such resources already at our command—with productions which control the commerce of the world—who can entertain any apprehensions as to our ability to succeed?[3]

Misguided Confidence

On April 12, 1861, Confederate forces fired on Fort Sumter, held by Union troops in South Carolina. The attack marked the opening rounds of the war. South Carolina socialite and author Mary Chesnut wrote soon thereafter, "Virginia and North Carolina are arming to come to our

Union and Confederate States of the Civil War

rescue, for now the North will swoop down on us. Of that we may be sure. We have burned our ships. We are obliged to go on now."[4]

Chesnut had reservations about fighting, but most Southerners went to war in 1861 confident that they would win. They were willing to fight to the death to preserve their homes, families, and way of life and felt they possessed bravery, patriotism, and determination superior to Northerners, whom they often referred to as Yankees. They considered Yankees paid agents of the government who lacked the commitment to fight intelligently and wholeheartedly.

Despite their confidence, Southerners ignored a critical factor that placed them at a disadvantage. In 1860 the North's total population exceeded 22 million, while the total population of the Confederate states was just over 9 million. Half of that number were slaves, and a good proportion of the rest were women and children. In essence, that meant that the South could put only half the number of soldiers in the field as the Union could, and Confederate armies would always be much smaller than Northern ones.

"The Lord Is on Our Side"

There were other factors that gave the North an advantage over the Confederacy. The latter had only 10 percent of the industrial capacity of the North, so it could not immediately produce war materiel such as cannons and rifles. Before the war, it had relied heavily on foreign trade, both as a market for its cotton and as a source of imports of necessities such as food, medicine, and manufactured goods. The Union naval blockade of Southern ports, which lasted from 1861 to 1865, was able to cut off such trade, which effectively crippled the Southern economy.

WORDS IN CONTEXT

black Republican

A derisive term for a member of the Republican Party who supported abolition and black equality.

Transportation was inferior in the South as well. The railroad network was disjointed, characterized by tracks that were different widths apart. This made it difficult to quickly transport troops and supplies to the front. Historian Shelby Foote summarized the situation by saying: "The North fought [the] war with one hand behind its back. . . . I think that if there had been more southern victories . . . the North simply would have brought that other arm out from behind its back. I don't think the South ever had a chance to win that war."[5]

In 1860, however, few Confederates understood the hopelessness of the effort. And thus they set forth enthusiastically, sacrificially, and—because most were Christians—prayerfully in the belief that they were destined to win. After all, they were trusting God and carrying out what they thought was God's will. That put them in the right, as one soldier, William Maxey of Georgia, confidently said. "We always will gain victory, for I believe the Lord is on our side."[6]

Chapter One

The Burden of Leadership

The states that formed the Confederacy in 1861 were united in their conviction that the US Constitution guaranteed them the right to secede—leave the Union—if they so desired. Based on that unity, life under the Confederate government ought to have been a time of undivided agreement. Participants were finally free to put their long-held philosophical beliefs about slavery and states' rights into practice. Although each state wanted to be independent, their decision to band together seemed a smart compromise so that they would have as much strength as possible to fight against powerful Union armies. The men who were chosen to lead the Confederacy seemed good choices, too. Most were former US senators and representatives, elected for their ability to lead and carry out the will of the people.

Seceding, writing a constitution, and electing new leaders were difficult but attainable tasks. Making the details of government work proved almost impossible, however. Some statesmen were conservative and clashed with those who held more radical views. Some held personal and political grudges against each other that hindered cooperation. Almost all were ignorant of how to run a new government and fight a war at the same time. As a result, their bickering and bad decision making hampered progress and eventually helped lead to the Confederacy's downfall.

Choosing a Capital

One of the first disagreements arose when leaders had to decide where the capital of the Confederacy would be located. The first choice of some was Montgomery, Alabama, home of the temporary capital. However,

Montgomery was hot and humid in the summer and offered limited lodging and restaurants for government officials.

There were other cities that were eager to open their doors to the government. Leaders of Atlanta, Georgia, and Nashville, Tennessee, for instance, promoted the climate and accommodations of their cities. So did leaders of Columbia, South Carolina. Even small towns offered their services. The editor of the *Upson Pilot* in little Thomaston, Georgia, wrote, "We have a fine climate, a productive country, and a virtuous and intelligent population. . . . We can supply all the officers of the government with old bacon and fresh greens and a cigar and bottle of old Bourbon or Tice's Best [whiskey] on Saturday nights."[7]

When Richmond, Virginia, was proposed as the capital, officials from states in the lower South objected because the state had been one of the last to secede. However, Richmond had distinct advantages. It was the Virginia state capital, and with a population of about thirty-eight thousand, it was the third-largest city of the Confederacy. It was a transportation hub with railroads and a port. It was also positioned close to the northern border of the Confederacy. Proponents hoped its selection would inspire other border states to follow Virginia out of the Union.

The Heart of the Confederacy

Once chosen as the capital, Richmond became the center of political and military affairs. It was not surprising to see congressmen, cabinet members, and heroes, such as Confederate general Robert E. Lee or cavalry legend Jeb Stuart on the street. Political hostess Virginia Clay-Clopton noted, "I remember on one occasion seeing President [Jefferson] Davis passing down the street, beside him, on the left, General [Simon B.] Buckner; on the right, General [John C.] Breckenridge—three stalwart and gallant men as ever walked abreast."[8]

By 1863 the city had grown to more than one hundred thousand people and was constantly abustle with soldiers, slaves, government workers, and refugees from the nearby countryside who needed protection and support. It also had more than its share of saloons, gambling halls, and houses of prostitution. Author Ernest B. Furgurson writes, "Richmond was by far the most expensive, corrupt, overcrowded, and crime-ridden city in the Confederacy."9

Spectators gather in 1861 in Montgomery, Alabama, for the inauguration of the Confederacy's president, Jefferson Davis. Differences of opinion, political grudges, and the reality of simultaneously running a new government and fighting a war posed huge challenges for the South's leaders.

Being the symbolic center of the Confederacy also made the capital a prime target during the war. It was less than 100 miles (161 km) south of the Union capital, Washington DC. Northern leaders realized that its capture would undermine morale and perhaps deal a death blow to the rebellion. Thus, Northern generals laid repeated plans to capture it; "On to Richmond" was the rallying cry of Union supporters. Richmond residents grew used to hearing the sound of cannons in the distance, and Clay-Clopton writes, "With the knowledge that we were in the city which, more than any other, invited and defied the attacks of the enemy, a sense of danger spurred our spirits. . . . The boom of guns was often not a distant sound."[10]

Talking and Fighting

Although life in the new Confederate capital was exciting, members of the government had an uphill struggle as they tried to do business. They came from different states and were not necessarily friends or even allies. Many had been hesitant to serve, either because they had not wholeheartedly supported secession or because they had hoped to fight in the war. And when they finally met together, they discovered that there was an impossible amount of work to be done—everything from creating a budget to setting up a postal service. There were no political parties with which members could align and form partnerships, so each man pushed his own agenda according to his own views.

As a result, men regularly quarreled and even got into physical fights. During a debate in 1863 over forming the Confederate Supreme Court, Alabama statesman William L. Yancey went so far as to reach for his gun, which caused Georgia senator Benjamin H. Hill to strike him with an inkstand. Mississippi senator Henry S. Foote was almost stabbed by Alabama congressman Edmund S. Dargan after interrupting one of Dargan's speeches and later had to be restrained from shooting Tennessee

In Their Own Words

"Poor Fools!"

Only a few Southern leaders recognized the mistake the South was making in seceding from the United States. Eliza Frances Andrews's father, Judge Garnett Andrews, was one, and in her diary, *The War-Time Journal of a Georgia Girl, 1864–1865*, she recalls his reaction when that state left the Union in 1861.

> Although he had retired from public life at the time, [my father] was elected to the legislature in 1860 under rather unusual circumstances; for the secession sentiment in the county was overwhelming, and his unwavering opposition to it well known. He did his best to hold Georgia in the Union, but he might as well have tried to tie up the northwest wind in the corner of a pocket handkerchief. . . .
>
> I shall never forget that night when the news came that Georgia had seceded. While the people of the village were celebrating the event with bonfires and bell ringing and speech making, he shut himself up in his house, darkened the windows, and paced up and down the room in the greatest agitation. Every now and then, when the noise of the shouting and the ringing of bells would penetrate to our ears through the closed doors and windows, he would pause and exclaim: "Poor fools! They may ring their bells now, but they will wring their hands—yes, and their hearts, too—before they are done with it."

Eliza Frances Andrews, *The War-Time Journal of a Georgia Girl, 1864–1865.* New York: D. Appleton, 1908, p. 184.

congressman William Swan after Swan struck Foote with an umbrella. Mary Chesnut, whose husband helped draft the Confederate constitution, became so irked that she questioned the wisdom of being part of a republic (representative government): "Republics, everybody jawing, everybody putting their mouths in, nothing sacred, all confusion of babble, crimination and recrimination—republics can't carry on war."[11]

Faced with so many difficulties, some men opted to leave their posts. That meant new appointments had to be made or members had to be shifted from one position to another. For instance, when Secretary of State Robert Toombs left office a few weeks into the war, his position was temporarily held by Robert M.T. Hunter and then by William M. Browne. When the permanent government went into operation in February 1862, Judah P. Benjamin, the first Jew to hold a cabinet-level office in the United States or the Confederacy, became secretary of state. Benjamin proved to be one of the most talented and flexible members of the cabinet. He served in three positions at different times—attorney general, secretary of war, and secretary of state.

A Flawed Leader

For those who served in government, Confederate president Jefferson Davis was a significant source of difficulty. Most men grudgingly admitted that he was the most qualified Southerner to be president. No one else in the South could match his combined military, political, and administrative experience. He was a graduate of West Point military academy and a veteran of the Mexican-American War of 1846. He had also served as a US senator from Mississippi and the US secretary of war. Lee commented after the war, "I don't think anyone could name anyone who could have done a better job than Jefferson Davis did."[12]

Yet Davis had habits and personality characteristics that irritated people and undermined his leadership. A highly reserved man, he seemed unable or unwilling to understand the feelings of the people around him. Statesman Sam Houston of Texas thought him "as cold as a lizard."[13] The trait alienated even his friends and kept him from winning their support when he needed it.

Davis also had the unfortunate tendency to hold grudges. Whenever others disagreed with him, he took their disagreements as personal attacks and became spiteful. In the words of newspaper owner Robert Barnwell Rhett Sr., he was "egotistical, arrogant, and vindictive."[14] He was also stubborn, and he had a habit of appointing his friends to positions in government and the military, even if they were poorly qualified.

Distracted by War

These were not Davis's only faults. His cabinet could count on the fact that he would be late for appointments and slow to make decisions. He was distracted by his many responsibilities and gave personal attention to issues that his clerks should have handled, such as attending to the thousands of letters that crossed his desk. He debated the pros and cons of everything from requests from soldiers wanting transfers to suggestions from inventors for building cannons, elevators, and primitive airplanes.

Despite the demands of government, however, his first interest was the war. He took time to make frequent trips to battlefronts. When there, he sometimes needlessly risked his life by getting too close to the front, as when he came under fire at the Battle of Seven Pines in 1862.

Intent on directing the war, he personally handled the placement of head generals and earned criticism for his involvement in their decision making. He defended underperforming generals, such as Braxton Bragg and John C. Pemberton, and allowed generals like Pierre Beauregard and Joseph E. Johnston to feud with each other to the detriment of their performance. When others urged him to appoint a general in chief of the Confederate army, he resisted. Lee was not appointed to that position until the last year of the war.

> **WORDS IN CONTEXT**
>
> **conscription**
>
> Compulsory enrollment of persons into the military; a draft.

Government Critics

Even if Davis had been a faultless leader, he would have earned criticism, thanks to his position as head of a government made up of states seek-

Jefferson Davis (seated, fourth from left) and his cabinet meet with General Robert E. Lee (standing, center). Although Davis had military, political, and administrative experience, his actions often frustrated colleagues including members of his cabinet.

ing to protect their individual rights and prerogatives. Any proposals he made to help coordinate war efforts were met with suspicion. Governor Zebulon Vance of North Carolina disputed his right to arrest North Carolina citizens who were suspected of disloyalty. Senator Foote and Georgia governor Joseph E. Brown even charged him with being part of a secret conspiracy to destroy individual liberty. Foote later recalled: "I did not intend to let Mr. Davis become an emperor if I could prevent it; nor allow his servitors [supporters] . . . to organize a military despotism in Richmond upon the false pretext that they were extreme devotees of state's rights and Southern independence."[15]

Throughout the war, Brown in particular did everything he could to thwart Davis's authority. For instance, when Davis asked for weapons from Georgia that could be used in other states, Brown withheld them. When Davis called for a national day of fasting and prayer, Brown ignored it, then called a different day of his own. He stated, "I entered into this Revolution to . . . sustain the rights of states and prevent the consolidation of the Government . . . no matter who may be in power."[16]

Davis had opponents even in his own cabinet. Volatile, outspoken secretary of state Toombs had hoped to become president of the Confederacy, so he resented Davis from the beginning. He also criticized Davis's policies, such as his decision to attack Fort Sumter. Davis largely ignored Toombs, which only added to his ill will. Davis also ignored Vice President Alexander Stephens, a highly sensitive, ambitious man who had expected to have a great deal of power as a leader of the Confederacy. Stephens retaliated by calling Davis "weak and vacillating [indecisive], timid, petulant, peevish, obstinate,"[17] and gave only halfhearted allegiance to him throughout the war.

Drowning in a Sea of Money

At the same time that members of government were hampered by internal problems, they also faced complicated issues that were vital to the new confederacy's survival. One of the most pressing was that of establishing a new system of money. After separating from the Union, the South did not want to use US currency, so Secretary of the Treasury Christopher G. Memminger was given the job of setting up and running a Confederate treasury. Memminger was a lawyer and did not understand public finance, but he did his best. He directed the Confederate-held federal mints in New Orleans, Louisiana, and Charlotte, North Carolina, to begin printing Confederate currency. With a shortage of precious metals, most of the money was not backed by hard assets, but by the promise of the Confederate government to redeem it after the war.

At first, Confederate currency had high purchasing power throughout the South. But as Southern enthusiasm waned and unscrupulous individuals began counterfeiting and passing Confederate money, its value dropped. To add to the problem, the government kept printing more to pay soldiers and suppliers for what it owed them. The result was runaway inflation—a rise in prices so that more money was necessary to make purchases. Biographer William J. Cooper Jr. observed, "The printing presses ran faster and faster, eventually pouring out a paper money

Looking Back

A Different World

The most controversial policy the Confederate government ever considered was that of enlisting slaves as soldiers to help win the war. The proposal challenged Southern notions of black inferiority, as author William J. Cooper Jr. points out in his book *Jefferson Davis, American.*

> Arming slaves and sending them into combat would have meant a fundamental uprooting of the traditional southern worldview. . . . The antebellum [before the war] proslavery argument placed blacks beneath whites racially and socially. To have them fight would give them characteristics of manhood previously denied them and put them on an equal basis with whites. . . . As teamsters, cooks, and laborers, slaves surely helped the Confederate war effort, but in these capacities they served in distinctly inferior roles. The white men did the fighting. But with slaves as combat soldiers the sharp distinction between superior and inferior could no longer hold. Combat service also brought up the question of freedom. Would slaves fight to maintain slavery, or would freedom become a requisite badge for bearing arms? . . . If becoming a soldier led to becoming a free man, then certainly the postbellum [postwar] social order would markedly differ from the world southern whites and blacks had always known.

William J. Cooper Jr., *Jefferson Davis, American.* New York: Knopf, 2000, p. 515.

avalanche of $1.5 billion. States and even localities also issued their own notes. . . . The Confederacy literally drowned in a sea of paper money. President Davis never comprehended the dimensions of the disaster."[18]

Faced with the fear of not being able to afford what they needed, many people began hoarding supplies. The *Richmond Enquirer* reported on one planter who had accumulated supplies until "the lawn and paths looked like a wharf covered with a ship's loads."[19] Others hoarded with an eye toward selling and making a profit when prices went higher. Their hoarding helped create shortages that made goods more valuable and added to inflation. Flour that cost $6 a barrel in 1861 sold for $500 a barrel in 1865. Bacon went from 12.5 cents a pound to $9 a pound. Coffee, which had been 35 cents a pound, rose to $60 a pound and was often simply unavailable.

> **WORDS IN CONTEXT**
> **forage**
> To search for food and other provisions.

"Rich Man's War, Poor Man's Fight"

Not only did the government face criticism over its management of the economy, it grew increasingly unpopular as it pushed through other policies it thought necessary to help win the war. One of the first was the Conscription Act of 1862, which stated that all healthy white men between the ages of eighteen and thirty-five had to serve three years in the military. In 1864 the age range was expanded to seventeen and fifty. The act authorized the first American draft in North America and was necessary because Confederate soldiers had quickly grown tired of fighting and gone home, leaving the army in desperate straits.

Conscription was hated by most Southerners, who saw it as limiting their freedom. It was opposed in official circles—one-third of the Confederate House and one-fourth of the Senate voted against it. Stephens called it a very bad policy. A lower court in Georgia found it unconstitutional, while volunteers in the army scorned conscripted soldiers whom they saw as inferior fighters. An editorial in the *Raleigh Standard* promised: "If the civil law is to be trampled under foot . . . and every able-bodied man placed in the army from sixteen to sixty-five . . . if the rights of the States are to be ignored and swept away. . . *the people of North Carolina will take their own affairs into their own hands.*"[20]

To try to satisfy the critics, the government passed an exemption act, which allowed railroad workers, ministers, teachers, and others who filled important wartime jobs to avoid service. It allowed those who could afford to hire substitutes to do so and also excused planters who owned twenty or more slaves. Confederate soldier Sam R. Watkins observed, "A law was made by the Confederate States Congress about this time allowing every person who owned twenty negroes to go home. It gave us the blues; we wanted twenty negroes. Negro property suddenly became very valuable, and there was raised the howl of 'rich man's war, poor man's fight.'"[21]

One pressing need of the Confederacy was the establishment of a new system of money. Confederate currency (pictured) initially had high purchasing power in the South, but its value dropped as the war progressed.

Arming the Slaves

Although conscription laws made enemies for the Confederate government, the suggestion that slaves be armed to help win the war provoked even more anger. The proposal was a sign of the South's desperate need for men by 1864, and General Patrick R. Cleburne was the first to present the idea to the military. In a letter to the Confederate high command, he wrote:

> The immediate effect of the emancipation and enrollment of negroes on the military strength of the South would be: To enable us to have armies numerically superior to those of the North, and a reserve of any size we might think necessary; to enable us to take the offensive, move forward, and forage on the enemy. It would open to us in prospective another and almost untouched source of supply, and furnish us with the means of preventing temporary disaster, and carrying on a protracted struggle.[22]

Once the suggestion went public, many met it with outrage. Brigadier General Patton Anderson called it a "monstrous proposition."[23] North Carolina senator William Graham insisted that arming slaves was highly dangerous; they would be likely to turn on white Confederates and kill them. General Howell Cobb of Georgia pointed out that the proposal was the direct opposite of everything the Confederacy stood for. "You cannot make soldiers of slaves, or slaves of soldiers. . . . And if slaves seem good soldiers, then our whole theory of slavery is wrong."[24]

After some deliberation, however, there were those who thought the idea was worthwhile. Lee, for instance, stated that it was a necessity if the South wanted to win the war. One unnamed slaveholder who wrote to the *Mobile Advertiser* in November 1864 said: "I am firmly convinced that public sentiment is in favor of putting our negroes in the army. I hear it expressed daily by those who own slaves and those who do not. . . . I feel sure that before the next meeting of Congress the propriety [correctness] . . . and necessity of arming the negroes will have taken hold on the public mind, that it will be advocated by a majority of our representatives."[25]

Downfall

His prediction was correct. Faced with the inevitable, on March 13, 1865, the Confederate Congress reluctantly passed a bill that authorized slaves to fight in the war. Before it could be implemented, however, it became clear that the end of the war was near. Secretary of State Benjamin later spoke for the entire government when he referred to "the anxious hours when we could not but perceive that our holy and sacred cause was gradually crumbling under a pressure too grievous to be borne."[26]

In April 1865 Lee and his forces could no longer hold back the thousands of Union soldiers who were advancing on Richmond. They retreated, leaving the city unprotected. Davis and what remained of the government desperately gathered their files and important papers and left on a train to Danville, Georgia, southwest of the capital. After Lee surrendered at Appomattox Courthouse in Virginia on April 9, Davis and the others fled to Greensboro, North Carolina, then on to Charlotte, South Carolina, and points beyond.

Without a capital or a government left to run, the war was soon over for them all. Stephens was arrested by Union troops at his home in Crawfordville, Georgia, on May 11, 1865, and served five months in prison. Memminger escaped arrest, but his homes and property were seized by the government. Toombs and Benjamin managed to escape to Europe, but Davis was captured by Union troops outside of Irwinville, Georgia, on May 10, 1865. He was taken north to Fortress Monroe off the coast of Virginia, charged with treason, and imprisoned for two years. Over that time, Southerners' respect for and loyalty to him grew as he staunchly refused to admit that the Confederacy had been wrong. Confederate soldier and author John S. Wise expressed the views of many when he said, "I never believed he was a very great man, or even the best President the Confederate States might have had. But he was our President. Whatever shortcomings he may have had . . . he did his best, to the utmost of his ability, for the Southern cause."[27]

Chapter Two

"This Is Soldiering"

For the almost 1 million Southern men who fought for the Confederacy, life during the Civil War was a mixture of adventure and hardship. The average "rebel," as he was known in the North, was middle class, poorly educated, and prejudiced against blacks. About one-third who served were between eighteen and twenty-five years of age. Fewer than half owned slaves. Early in the war most were especially eager for the chance to defend their home state. They had seldom been far from home before, so the chance to travel, see new sights, and pit their fighting skills against the enemy was irresistible.

On the other hand, their lives and loyalties had always revolved around their families, and they hated to leave them unsupported and unprotected. As homesickness combined with the realities of war—cold, hunger, and boredom interrupted by the repeated risk of death—their support for the war changed. Confederate soldier Sam R. Watkins recalled, "We soon found out that the glory of war was at home . . . and not upon the field of blood and carnage and death, where our comrades were mutilated and torn by shot and shell."[28]

Preparing to Leave

When war was declared, volunteers across the South began forming units and companies, often even before they had authorization from military authorities. Filled with romantic notions, they liked to choose names for themselves that they believed reflected their fierceness, such as the Baker Fire Eaters, Tallapoosa Thrashers, Chickasaw Desperados, and Southern Avengers.

Because there were no uniforms yet designed for this new army, volunteers provided their own clothing. Many men simply wore the clothes they owned—homespun gray shirts, nondescript trousers, and boots or heavy shoes. Sometimes a rich patron in the neighborhood supplied money for uniforms, which were sewn by volunteer seamstresses. There was no coordination of styles until later in the war when the government supplied standard-issue gray outfits, so some units, like the Emerald Guards of Mobile, Alabama, had earlier worn dark green uniforms. A company of East Tennesseans known as the Yellow Jackets wore all yellow. The Louisiana Zouaves were the most stylish, with red, baggy trousers, blue sashes, jackets decorated with braid and lace, and Middle Eastern–style fezzes on their heads.

The government had no prearranged contracts with suppliers of horses, knives and guns, so men supplied their own—particularly their own horse if they owned one. If a soldier's horse was injured or killed during the war, the soldier was responsible for replacing it at his own expense. More men had guns than horses, but many lacked modern rifles and had to make do with shotguns, squirrel rifles, and vintage muskets. This proved a great hindrance in battle, as historian Bell Irwin Wiley notes: "At the battle of Mill Springs, Kentucky, January 19, 1862, the Confederates were hampered by the fact that rain made unusable the flintlock rifles with which many of the regiments were outfitted. Some of the Tennesseans, after several futile attempts to fire their dampened pieces, were seen to break them in exasperation over a near-by rail fence."[29] Once into battle, men supplemented weapon shortages by scrounging from dead Yankees who were better equipped by the US Army. It was not until early 1863 that enough rifles were being manufactured to adequately supply Southern soldiers in battle.

> **WORDS IN CONTEXT**
> **homespun**
> Cloth made at home or made of yarn spun at home.

Off to War

As they prepared to leave home, units were treated to farewell banquets, speeches, commitment ceremonies at church, and the like. Then on the day of departure, family, neighbors, and friends gathered either at the local railroad station or the town square to load the men down with parting gifts of food and drink and to say goodbye. Many soldiers had never been away from home or ridden a train before, so the journey itself was exciting. As they traveled, they yelled and sang and climbed on top of the cars for a good view of the countryside. Crowds waved at them and cheered as they passed through towns. Wiley says, "When they rode in boxcars, the occupants often used the butts of their guns to knock holes in the sides for ventilation and sight-seeing, and as they rode along yelling and singing, with their heads sticking out of the openings, they reminded onlookers of chickens in a poultry wagon."[30]

Members of the 5th Georgia Infantry Regiment pose outside their tent during the Civil War. Early in the war, most Confederate soldiers lacked uniforms. Many wore shirts, pants, and shoes brought from home.

Once the early excitement was over, being in the army turned out to be different from what most men had imagined. They had looked forward to their first battle with an eager spirit. Confident in their fighting abilities, they did not believe that the enemy would be difficult to defeat. Therefore, most believed that the war would be short, and they would miss the chance to fight if they did not hurry. Watkins remembered his disappointment when he and a group of new recruits arrived at Manassas (called Bull Run by Northerners) too late to take part in the first battle of the war. "Ah, how we envied those that were wounded. We thought at that time that we would have given a thousand dollars to have been in the battle, and to have had our arm shot off, so we could have returned home with an empty sleeve. But the battle was over, and we left out."[31]

In fact, most discovered that the war would last longer than expected and much of their time would be spent in boring, everyday routine. First they spent time drilling, learning to follow orders, move in formation, and operate weapons. They then endured long marches to get to the front. If they had to retreat after a battle, they walked again over the same ground. In 1863 General Robert E. Lee's army marched almost 150 miles (241 km) to cover ground between one battle near Chancellorsville, Virginia, and the next in Gettysburg, Pennsylvania. Watkins recalls the long treks he and his fellow soldiers endured: "We were ever on the march—tramp, tramp, tramp—always on the march."[32]

First Battle

All the monotony disappeared when men actually went into battle. In the silence before the first cannons fired, many thought of their families or prayed that God would keep them safe through the fighting. When bullets and cannon balls actually began whistling overhead, some panicked and ran away. Others cowered on the ground, horrified by the blood and falling bodies. Most, however, felt their tension ease as they took action. They became calmer and more purposeful, repeatedly loading their weapons, moving forward, and firing. Lieutenant S.G. Pryor recalled after his first fight, "It was a pretty severe anniciation (initiation) the test was severe but thank god I had the nerve to stand it."[33]

In the confusion of battle, men usually gave no thought to strategy or tactics. Watkins observed, "'Steady, double quick, charge bayonets, fire at will,' is about all that a private soldier ever knows of a battle. He can see the smoke rise and the flash of the enemy's guns, and he can hear the whistle of the minnie [minié balls] and cannon balls, but he has got to load and shoot as hard as he can."[34]

Troops in the rear sometimes overran those in the front. Friendly fire, during which Southerners shot other Southerners out of confusion or poor aim, was common. Especially at the beginning of the war, many men found themselves in the midst of other regiments at the end of a day's fight. There had been so much blind running and ducking in dense smoke that everyone had gotten separated.

The Horror of War

Even for those who performed well, battles were traumatizing. Men rushed forward over bloody ground that was tangled with dead men and horses. Their comrades were blown apart or crumpled dead before their eyes. At the same time, they themselves killed others for the first time in their lives. One man wrote, "Civilized people killing one another like beasts one would think that the supreme ruler would put a stop to it."[35]

Nor did the horror stop at the battle's end. For hours afterward, the moans and cries of the wounded and dying on the field haunted those who survived. Sorting the wounded from the dead was a gruesome task that had to be done. The wounded had to be carried to field hospitals that were set up in the rear, and these were places of horror as well. Operations—usually amputations—were performed on makeshift tables and were extremely painful because of the shortage of pain-dulling medicine and the dullness of surgical tools. Arms and legs that were removed were simply piled to one side. Watkins described conditions in one hospital he visited: "Those hollow-eyed and sunken-cheeked

In Their Own Words

"I Will Stay in the Field Forever"

Many soldiers spent their spare time writing home, recalling more peaceful times before the war. Private Thomas D. Newton of the 8th Louisiana Infantry was no exception. The following is a portion of a letter sent to his sister in Virginia on May 28, 1862.

Sister Mary,

I will tell you how much I think of home. That delightful home I have so often thought of the greater portion of my day in quietude enjoying the pleasures and comforts of life, and those that are dear to me. . . . There is of home a delightful place where one can have peace, and just rights with it. But, without those two items death is far preferable. I will stay in the field forever before I will have my country invaded. I will submit to the toils and hardships of camp. I will be found traversing the snow-clad cliffs of the Thoroughfare and the Blue Ridge Mountains first. I will endure the toil, forbear the pain produced thereby, before thinking of submitting to such tyrannical vandals as those negro-thieving, undermining, careless, unprincipled band of demons, which are really beneath the notice of the Devil himself.

I say and speak from my heart that life is sweet, though give me death before submitting to any such. . . .

Nothing more remains,

your warrior brother, until death,

Thomas D. Newton

Quoted in *Home of the American Civil War*, "Letter from Private Thomas D. Newton, 8th Louisiana Infantry," May 28, 1862. www.civilwarhome.com.

sufferers, shot in every conceivable part of the body; some shrieking, and calling upon their mothers; some laughing the hard, cackling laugh of the sufferer without hope . . . and some writhing and groaning as their wounds were being bandaged and dressed."[36]

So great was the trauma of battle that many men had repeated nightmares and could not speak of what they had seen and done for days afterward. Others coped by writing letters home in which they expressed their feelings. Eventually most men became used to the horrors of the battlefield, but this hardening bothered some as well. After having seen a fellow soldier's arm ripped off by a shell, John T. Sibley wrote, "I am astonished at my own indifference. . . . It distresses me at times when I am cool and capable of reflection to think how indifferent we become in the hour of battle when our fellow men fall around us by scores. . . . My God what kind of a people will we be?"[37]

Camp Life

Between battles, much of life was spent in camp. Although it provided men opportunities to rest, camp life was not easy either. Willingly or not, most Confederates were examples of Confederate general Richard Ewell's policy: "The road to glory cannot be followed with much baggage."[38] They carried few supplies with them, often only a canteen, blanket, frying pan, and tin cup. They cooked over campfires, bathed if there was a convenient creek or river nearby, and slept on the ground in all weather. One officer observed in 1864, "The ground is too cold for them to lie down on, and their one blanket is not warm enough for them to cover with. This is soldiering, this is."[39]

With so little equipment, there was no way that they could be comfortable, especially because they were often hungry. Food was almost always in short supply, especially meat. Mule meat was substituted for beef, and men agreed that it was better than no meat at all, but any shipment from the military could be tough and stringy. One soldier remarked of his share that "buzzards would not eat it at any season of the year."[40] Other staple items were molasses, corn or cornmeal, and fat bacon, and these were used in a variety of ways. One common dish was known as "sloosh" or "cush" and made from a combination of bacon grease, water, and cornbread and cooked over a campfire. As one man wrote in October 1862, "If I ever lose my patriotism, and the 'secesh' [secessionist] spirit dies out then you may know the 'Commissary' [military food department] is at fault. Corn meal mixed with water and tough beef three times a day will knock the 'Brave Volunteer' under quicker than Yankee bullets."[41]

To round out their scanty diets, men scavenged for what they could find. Greens and other fresh vegetables could sometimes be found in gardens they passed on their marches. Wild berries and nuts were plentiful in certain seasons and could be eaten while walking. Soldiers sometimes convinced sympathetic farmwives to cook them a meal, too, but with dozens of men traveling together, there was no possibility that all could be fed in this way.

WORDS IN CONTEXT
sloosh
Also called cush; food made of bacon grease, cornbread, and water, cooked over a campfire.

Passing the Time

Between cooking and sleeping, there were many empty hours to be passed in camp, and soldiers did what they could to relieve the boredom. Many read the Bible or wrote to folks at home. One man's letter boasted of valuables he had captured after a battle: "I write to you on Yankee paper, with a gold pen, & Yankee envelope, with Yankee ink . . . full of Yankee sugar coffee."[42] Some whittled, crafting pipes out of corncobs or making small animals out of wood. Some amused themselves by playing pranks on their comrades. They might smoke a man out of his tent, load his firewood with gunpowder so it would go off with a small explosion, or steal his love letters and read them aloud. Stealing as a joke was common. For instance, one man who had been boiling a wild turkey returned to his fire to find only a feather floating in the pot.

Of the more wholesome pastimes, singing around the campfire in the evenings was a favorite. The men often sang songs about the war and the enemy, accompanied by musical instruments such as violins and guitars. On Sundays, some attended church services held by a military chaplain who traveled with them. In good weather many played baseball, and when it snowed, snowball fights were inevitable. These fights could last for several hours and be extremely rough. Men lost teeth, got black eyes and bloody noses, and in cases where snowballs were loaded with rocks or lead, were seriously injured or killed.

Some pastimes involved more daring pleasures that had perhaps been forbidden at home. Many men took up smoking for the first time. Others liked gambling and bet on anything from cards to louse races. Cash was scarce, so they staked whatever they might have, such as a pocket knife or an extra ration of food or clothing. Alcohol was usually in short supply, too, but men managed to satisfy their thirst by buying it from local bootleggers or camp followers. One frustrated lieutenant wrote, "A soldier will get whiskey at any risk—if anywhere in the neighborhood."[43] Along with drinking, men took an interest in women whenever they had a chance to meet them. There were always prostitutes who followed the army or who lived in towns that soldiers passed, and many men visited them regularly.

Fever and Fleas

Because they were poorly fed and constantly exposed to the elements, many soldiers fell ill, especially during the winter. Some caught colds that developed into bronchitis and pneumonia. Others suffered from dysentery and food poisoning. Country boys who had not been exposed to childhood diseases were susceptible to measles, mumps, typhoid fever, and influenza. Private J.W Love wrote to his family in August 1862, "They have Been 11 Died with the fever in Co A since we left kinston [North Carolina] and 2 died that was wounded so you now See that these Big Battles is not as Bad as the fever."[44] All in all, the crowded camps were breeding grounds for disease, and twice as many men died of disease during the war as did those who died of gunshot wounds.

In addition to illness, men constantly battled pests such as fleas, lice, and mosquitos, which could carry malaria. All were uncontrollable because men slept outdoors and did not bathe often. One man testified that

With food and equipment in short supply, camp life for Confederate soldiers held few comforts. Even so, soldiers found ways to occupy their time, including practicing their knife-throwing skills, as depicted in this illustration of Mississippi soldiers in a Confederate army camp.

"they [fleas] collect in companies at knight fall for the purpose of carrying us off . . . though like the Yankeys they are repulsed by desperate efforts & great patience."[45] The itch of body lice and fleas was maddening, so during periods of rest, men passed the time picking them from their clothes, beards, or scalp. Georgia native Eliza Frances Andrews wrote of the men she observed, "These men were, most of them, born gentlemen, and there could be no more pitiful evidence of the hardships they have suffered than the lack of means to free themselves from these disgusting creatures."[46]

Treatments for disease were primitive at the time, and medicine was scarce. Camp doctors generally had little more than opium or morphine for pain, quinine for malaria, and blue mass (a pill or syrup made of a mixture of mercury, licorice, and other ingredients) for other ailments. When those ran short, everyone relied on herbal or home remedies. These could range from slippery elm or sweet gum tea for diarrhea and malaria to mustard plasters for chest complaints. A mixture of vinegar and salt was taken to cure coughs. Fresh pennyroyal (a member of the mint family) or peach leaves placed in the bed were thought to ward off fleas, while an ointment made of white elder flower, sulfur, and peppermint oil apparently reduced itch.

"Mighty Rough"

After months of hunger, fear, illness, homesickness, and high casualties, many men decided that they no longer wanted to fight in the war. Conscription—the government draft—only stirred their resentment. Watkins writes, "A law had been passed by the Confederate States Congress called the conscript act. . . . From this time on till the end of the war, a soldier was simply a machine, a conscript. It was mighty rough on rebels. . . . All our pride and valor had gone, and we were sick of war and the Southern Confederacy."[47]

Letters from loved ones at home offered good arguments for leaving the army. Mary Epperly of Floyd County, Virginia, wrote to her husband: "Dear Marion I do wish that you would all come home for it looks like as long as you all stay thare [there] and fight they wont try to make pease [peace] and if you would all leaves they would be obliged to do something it just looks to me like they will keeep the men thare till thare [they're] all killed."[48]

> **WORDS IN CONTEXT**
> **mustard plaster**
> Mustard seed powder moistened with water or egg and placed in a protective bandage and applied to the chest or back.

The fact that soldiers were not being paid for their service added to their unhappiness. Lee wrote in 1865, "Insufficiency of food and non-payment of the troops have more to do with the dissatisfaction . . . than anything else."[49]

"We Had Seen It All"

Even those men who remained out of loyalty to their commander wavered when they learned that a change of leadership was taking place. When Watkins broke the news to his fellow soldiers that beloved general

Looking Back

All Heroes

Historian Shelby Foote, who died in 2005, was a Southerner as well as an expert on the Civil War. In an article titled "Men at War," Foote provides little-known information on the democratic practices of the Confederate army.

> There were no medals awarded in the Confederate army—not one in the whole course of the war. The Confederate reason for that was that they were all heroes and it would not do to single anyone out. They were not all heroes, of course. But when the suggestion was made to [General Robert E.] Lee that there be a roll of honor for the Army of Northern Virginia, Lee disallowed it. The highest honor you could get in the Confederate army was to be mentioned in dispatches. And that was considered absolutely enough.

Quoted in Geoffrey C. Ward, Ric Burns, and Ken Burns, *The Civil War: An Illustrated History.* New York: Knopf, 1990, p. 267.

Joseph E. Johnston had been replaced by General John Bell Hood in mid-1864, many threw down their guns and left. Watkins wrote, "They marched off, and it was the last we ever saw of them. In ten minutes they were across the river. . . . Such was the sentiment of the army of Tennessee at that time."[50]

By the end of the war, men were deserting in large numbers. In February 1865 there were more than one hundred thousand desertions recorded throughout the Confederacy, with thousands more unrecorded. Some men slipped away from their camps in the night. Some straggled away from the end of the line while they were marching. It is estimated that fewer than 175,000 men remained when Lee surrendered to Union general Ulysses S. Grant on April 9, 1865.

Although surrender and defeat was humiliating, all who remained had the proud knowledge that they had persevered to the end. Even those who deserted were conscious that they had been part of a once-in-a-lifetime experience. Watkins observed, "We had seen and felt the pleasure of the life of a soldier. . . . Yes, we had seen it all, and had shared in its hopes and fears; its love and its hate; its good and its bad; its virtue and its vice; its glories and its shame. We had followed the successes and reverses of the flag of the Lost Cause through all these years of blood and strife."[51]

Chapter Three

Isolated and Afraid

Because the South was a rural, agrarian society, the majority of Southerners were farm people. About 5 percent were planters who lived on large estates and owned twenty or more slaves. The rest lived on some fifty thousand medium-size plantations across the region, as well as innumerable small farms where home was a log cabin and the family raised corn, chickens, and a few hogs for their own use. They owned few or no slaves.

No matter what their social status, when men went off to war, women, children, and the elderly were left to carry on as best they could. Margaret Junkin Preston of Lexington, Virginia, described her neighborhood as "a world of femininity with a thin line of boys and octogenarians."[52] Women provided food and supplies for the troops, protected themselves from dangers ranging from starvation to assault by the enemy, and took on new management and leadership roles. They did all this while coping with loneliness and the fear that they would never see their loved ones again. The stress produced lasting and irreparable changes. As Lucy Buck of Front Royal, Virginia, observed in her diary in 1862, "We shall never any of us be the same as we have been."[53]

Feminine and Patriotic

Before the war, Southern women were seldom seen as leaders of the family. They had been guided and protected by their husbands and fathers and were expected to marry, have children, and take care of the home. In almost all cases they were excluded from decision making and had little to do with supervising slaves, if the family owned any. Living in the country, most were used to isolation because homes were far apart. The nearest neighbors were far across the fields. The nearest town might be hours away, and respectable women did not travel without a male escort.

After plantation wife Anne Nichols moved to her husband's Virginia estate, she wrote that she was "absolutely as far removed from everything . . . as if I was in a solitary tomb."[54]

Even though the war had robbed them of the companionship, leadership, and protection they were used to, most women were fiercely patriotic, particularly in the early years. Many pushed their men to volunteer and shamed them when they hesitated. Kate Cumming, the daughter of a wealthy Southern merchant, stated that a man "did not deserve the name of man if he did not fight for his country."[55] Some were even frustrated that they were not men, so badly did they want to fight. And although they were anxious about what would happen when their men left, they hid those fears. New bride Priscilla M. Bond of Louisiana wrote in her diary, "How I do hate to give him up, but I suppose I have to be a martyr during this war."[56]

Whether they had men in the army or not, women across the South almost immediately realized that they needed to provide support for those who were on the battlefield. They instinctively turned to doing what they were good at—cooking and sewing—to make sure that their men were as well cared for as possible. Catherine Edmondston of North Carolina helped organize efforts in her neighborhood and recalled, "Never was there known such unanimity of action amongst all classes."[57]

Care Packages

The women did their best to provide meals and a place to sleep to any Confederate soldiers who passed their way. At the same time, they created care packages, which they sent to those at the front. In the first years of the war, there was no shortage of food on farms, so everything from potatoes and meat to pies, cakes, and cookies went into the bundles. One wife sent her husband his favorite apple butter, sausages, and chestnuts. Because the mail was unreliable, packages were often sent with servants, relatives, or soldiers returning to the front. Many packages were lost in transit, but the ones that arrived were greatly appreciated. Private T.B.

In Their Own Words

Invaders

To isolated women on plantations, most black men—slaves or runaways—were frightening. Louisiana native Kate Stone describes her feelings during an event that occurred near the family plantation, Brokenburn, in northeastern Louisiana in 1862.

> Looking out of the window we saw three fiendish-looking black Negroes standing around [our friend] George Richards, two with their guns level and almost touching his breast. . . . We thought he would be killed instantly, and I shut my eyes that I might not see it. But after a few words from George, which we could not hear, and another volley of curses, they lowered their guns and rushed into the house "to look for guns" they said, but only to rob and terrorize us. The Negroes were completely armed and there was no white man with them. We heard them ranging all through the house, cursing and laughing and breaking things open.

Quoted in John Q. Anderson, ed., *Brokenburn: The Journal of Kate Stone, 1861–1868.* Baton Rouge: Louisiana State University Press, 1955, p. 195.

Hampton enthused in a letter to his wife: "The Butter and Honey was . . . devoured with as much ferocity as a wolf would devour a sheep."[58]

Women also made clothing that they included in care packages. The Union blockade meant that they could not use imported fabric, buttons, or trims, but many owned spinning wheels and looms and were used to making their own cloth. Those who did not know how to sew soon learned. Georgia native and author Mary Gay remembered, "Many of us who had never learned to sew became expert handlers of the needle."[59] Fabric was dyed with color that came from plants such as onions, carrots, dandelion roots, or oak bark, so many soldiers wore earth tones such as butternut brown rather than standard-issue gray.

As often as they wove new cloth, women used and reused fabric, buttons, and ribbons they found around the house. Old clothes were dyed, cut, and sewn into new garments for soldiers, themselves, and their children. Curtains and sofa pillows were made into jackets. Scarves and aprons were pieced together to make shirts and blouses. One woman wrote, "It was not uncommon to see skirts that had been turned inside out, upside down and hind part before. I well remember one faithful old jaconet [cotton fabric], which after submitting to various alterations as dress and petticoat, was finally . . . cut up and hemmed for pocket handkerchiefs."[60]

New Responsibilities

In addition to traditional indoor activities, countrywomen had to take on a host of outdoor responsibilities that their husbands, fathers, and brothers had performed. Farmwives who had no servants or slaves did the plowing and planting. They also repaired gates, cut firewood, milked cows, and mucked out barns. This made their days extremely long and wearying, especially because they also had more conventional jobs such as tending gardens, preserving food for winter, and caring for their many children. When women had an average of seven or eight offspring, the burden of child raising was especially heavy during wartime. One woman wrote to a childless friend, "I think any one who is free from the 'little animals' can scarcely be thankful enough in these days of war. It is hard enough for a woman to take care of herself."[61]

Wives of wealthy planters did not often work in the fields, but they also had many children to care for in addition to supervising slaves. Most slaves were motivated to work only by the threat of force, and they recognized that, with a female in charge, that threat was less. Plantation wives were, for the most part, physically weaker than their husbands—and

Slaves pick cotton on a Southern plantation. The fear of slave uprisings was ever present among Southern women who were left to run plantations while their men were away at war.

many of the slaves. They were also not used to doling out punishments such as beatings and whippings. Thus, slaves often defied a woman's orders, and it was difficult for her to know what to do when that happened. Ellen Moore of Virginia wrote of her slaves, "All think I am a kind of usurper & have no authority over them."[62]

To cope with the problem, many women hired an overseer or persuaded an older male relative or neighbor to help them manage the plantation. When a man was not available, however, they simply dealt with the situation as best they could. Some stepped far out of their traditional feminine roles. For instance, Susan Scott of Texas confessed that she shouted curses at slaves when they failed to do their chores correctly. Emily Perkins of Tennessee directed her loyal slaves to tie down a defiant one so she could whip him. Some women avoided violence by bargaining—promising slaves better living conditions or more freedom to get them to work. Many, however, tried to ignore the defiance, afraid that their slaves would retaliate or run away if pushed too hard. "I was never half as sweet tempered in my life as I have been this year,"[63] admitted Georgian Leila Callaway in a letter to her husband.

Enemies Within

The fear that slaves might become violent was all too real for Southern women. They had been taught that male slaves were animalistic, sexually uncontrolled, and always ready to attack. Slaves were also numerous, strong, resentful of being mistreated, and aware that isolated rural women could be easy prey. Mrs. A. Ingraham of Vicksburg, Tennessee, stated, "I fear the blacks more than I do the Yankees."[64]

Reports of slave uprisings against women heightened everyone's fears. There were rumors of slaves sneaking into women's bedrooms. There were stories of murders, fires, and poisonings carried out by slaves. To back the rumors there were proven cases of violence. In 1861 a group of slaves near Natchez, Mississippi, was arrested just before they attacked the wives and daughters of prominent slaveholders in the neighborhood. That same year Mary Chesnut learned that one of her relatives, an elderly widow who lived alone, had been smothered by one of her female servants. Chesnut wrote: "Somehow today I feel that the ground is cut away from under my feet. Why should they treat me any better than they have done Cousin Betsey Witherspoon?"[65]

Overwhelmed by their fears, many women wrote letters to state and Confederate officials asking that they be given protection. If this was impossible, they requested that they be supplied with arms and ammunition so that they could defend themselves and, in the words of several women in Jasper County, Mississippi, "die with honor & innocence sustained."[66] There is no record that anyone responded to their requests, so most women continued to live in fear of attack from their slaves for the duration of the war.

Enemies from Outside

There were some Southern women who feared white Confederates more than they feared slaves. These were usually pacifist Quakers and those in border states whose male relatives would not fight or had decided to fight for the North. Left unprotected, they often had to hide or flee to escape being hunted down and killed by their zealous neighbors. North Carolinian Louisa Stiles, whose husband, two sons,

Looking Back

Keeping a Diary

Many important details of life in the South can be found in the diaries that women kept during the Civil War. As editor Drew Gilpin Faust explains in the introduction to *Brokenburn: The Journal of Kate Stone, 1861–1868*, such diaries served many purposes, including allowing isolated women to feel that they were doing something important during the conflict.

> Kate chaffed at being left behind when her male friends and relatives departed for the war in 1861. . . . "O! to see and be in it all," she lamented. "I hate weary days of inaction. . . ."
>
> Longing to be in the midst of historic events unfolding around her, Kate began a diary to claim that experience as her own. For Stone, as for hundreds of other Confederate women, diary keeping would provide a means of participating in the war, a way of resisting the marginalization [unimportance] they felt because of their exclusion as females from "the tented field." Writing was a form of action and involvement, a means of shaping events through words, even if not through more direct participation in what Kate called "the busy world outside."

Quoted in John Q. Anderson, ed., *Brokenburn: The Journal of Kate Stone, 1861–1868*. Baton Rouge: Louisiana State University Press, 1955, p. xxxii.

and two brothers joined the Union army, recalled that she and her children were often in danger because of their allegiance. She recalled, "I was often threatened with killing, and having my house burned, and property destroyed."[67]

More women trembled at the thought of Union troops on their property, however. As enemy forces passed through or captured different sections of the country, they did not hesitate to take shelter in homes along the way. When this happened, residents had to submit. They were no match for dozens of armed men who were intent on gaining entrance. Cornelia Peake McDonald wrote of the arrival of Union forces at her home near Winchester, Virginia, in 1862: "We were about to sit down to breakfast, when the house was surrounded by men who, with their fists began to break in the windows. . . . I rushed to the front of the house and

Members of a Virginia family refuse to abandon their home even after it has been bombarded and looted by soldiers of the Union army. Women left at home to care for children and elderly relatives endured theft, fire, and vandalism during the war.

shut and locked the hall door, but on opening the study door found that they had entered there by breaking in the windows, and were carrying off the few stores I had which had been put there . . . for safekeeping."[68]

McDonald and other women had to submit to pillaging, which was encouraged by Union generals to weaken resistance. Troops were allowed to steal valuables, break what they could not steal, burn fields, and even burn entire homes. Furniture such as pianos, beds, sofas, tables, and chairs were destroyed. Breakables such as vases, marble statues, and mirrors were smashed. Clothing was scattered. Carpets were trampled with mud. Poor non-slaveholding whites fared no better than richer ones. In the Shenandoah Valley, Union soldiers pillaged the property of poor white tenants (renters), whose shacks were sprinkled in between the small plantations.

"Like Famished Wolves"

To avoid total loss, Southerners attempted to hide food and articles of value when they heard that troops were approaching. Georgian Dolly Lunt Burge described her family's efforts:

> I went to the smoke-house, divided out the meat to the servants, and bid them hide it. Julia [a slave] took a jar of lard and buried it. In the meantime Sadai [Burge's daughter] was taking down and picking up our clothes, which she was giving to the servants to hide in their cabins; silk dresses, challis, muslins, and merinos, linens, and hosiery, all found their way into the chests of the women and under their beds; china and silver were buried underground.[69]

Such efforts were usually useless, however. Soldiers were skilled at finding hideaways, sometimes assisted by slaves who had helped to hide the valuables in the first place. Then women had to watch helplessly as gold and silver coins, silverware, jewelry, and heirlooms were loaded on the soldiers' saddles and taken away.

Often not everything could be hidden in time. Burge's home netted troops an enormous treasure trove of foodstuff, which she mourned losing:

> To my smoke-house, my dairy, pantry, kitchen, and cellar, like famished wolves they come, breaking locks and whatever is in their way. The thousand pounds of meat in my smoke-house is gone in a twinkling, my flour, my meat, my lard, butter, eggs . . . all gone. My eighteen fat turkeys, my hens, chickens, and fowls, my young pigs, are shot down in my yard and hunted as if they were rebels themselves.[70]

"I Was So Mad"

Although women feared Union troops and what they could do, their fears were somewhat eased by the hope that the Northerners were civilized enough to treat females with respect. Like Virginian Mary Lee, they "demanded the courtesy that every lady has the right to expect from every gentleman."[71] In most cases their hopes were well founded. Most Union soldiers were reluctant to harm women. There were instances where women were victimized, but few attacks occurred when an officer was present, and few upper-class women were targeted.

WORDS IN CONTEXT

challis

A soft, plainly woven fabric made of cotton or wool.

Once they saw that they were treated with respect, some women dared to express the anger and resentment they always felt in the presence of the enemy. Lee recalled, "I never had such feelings in my life. I was so mad I was trembling with passion."[72] Some women pointedly ignored the intruders, refusing to look at or speak to them even though they were everywhere in the house.

Others went a step farther. They quarreled with, spit at, and even hit the invaders. For instance, one woman pushed a soldier down the stairs when he tried to grab her dead brother's clothing out of her hands. Elizabeth McKamy of Tennessee snatched up a stick of wood and began beating a Union soldier when he took a slice of bread from her nephew.

"Dreadful and Deafening"

Southern women not only endured the enemy invading their homes, they sometimes found themselves on the edge of battle if the two sides happened to clash near at hand. McDonald described such an incident in March 1862: "An intervening hill shut out the sights but not the fearful sounds, which . . . became more dreadful and deafening till two o'clock in the afternoon; then the cannon ceased, and in its place the most terrible and long continued musketry firing, some said, that had been heard since the war began."[73]

As battles shifted, homes could come directly in the line of fire. Then families could only cower inside while cannon balls shrieked across yards, snapping off trees and smashing buildings. McDonald recalled a night when shells hurtled over her head and those of her children:

The children were leaning on my lap; I was holding my poor little Hunter. Roy and Nelly were perfectly composed, looking up at the shells as they flew over and came crashing down. Donald, poor little four-year-old baby, hid his face on my knee and sobbed. Old Aunt Winnie sat not far off, crying and wringing her hands. "Oh Miss Cornelia," she said, "you will all be killed." I did not know whether we would be or not, it really seemed impossible that we could come out of that chaos alive.[74]

Despite the danger, women often remained in their homes because running away seemed cowardly and unpatriotic. Then too, many could not afford to leave; they had nothing but their land and possessions. Georgian Sarah Espy, who had several children, wrote in 1863, "[I] feel more like trying to stay at home and take whatever Providence may send; I do not know where I could go, or how, with so large a family and no one to lead for us. It will be ruin to either go or stay, I fear."[75]

Refugees

Despite their desire to remain in their homes, many Southern women finally gave up, packed what they could carry, and fled. Those who had a wagon and mule were able to take some furniture with them while others took nothing but bundles of clothing and food. They traveled in any weather—hot sunshine or pouring rain—and camped along the roadside at night until they could find someplace to stay. McDonald wrote of her family's flight in 1863: "We were constantly in sight of, and often jostled by moving crowds of people and vehicles. Many wounded men were among them making their way to a place of safety, while fugitives of every grade and degree of misery were toiling on, on foot, or in any kind of broken-down vehicle."[76]

When they arrived at a town or other place of relative safety, those who were fortunate stayed with friends or acquaintances. Those with money hired a room in a hotel or boarding house if one was available. Accommodations were always overcrowded, however, and many were filthy and/or infested with fleas and bedbugs. Eliza Frances Andrews wrote of one room she shared with other women in her family after they fled to Scottsboro, Georgia:

> **WORDS IN CONTEXT**
> **slop tub**
> A basin for wastewater.

There was no slop tub, wash basin, pitcher nor towels, and the walls on each side of the beds were black with tobacco spit. The fireplace was a dump heap that was enough to turn the stomach of a pig, and over the mantel some former occupant had inscribed this caution: "One bed has lice in it, the other fleas, and both bugs; chimney smokes; better change."

Prompted by curiosity I turned down the cover of one bed, and started such a stampede among the bugs that we all made for the door as fast as our feet would carry us and ordered another room, which, however, did not prove much better.[77]

Many times multiple families camped out in abandoned buildings with holes in the ceiling and broken windows. Despite the shoddy conditions, these were overcrowded as well. Everyone slept on the floor and shared eating spaces with other families. For instance, after becoming a refugee from her home in Baton Rouge, Louisiana, Sarah Morgan Dawson found herself sharing a mattress on the floor with her female slave, a situation that would have been unthinkable for her before the war. She wrote: "To my share fell a double blanket, which, as Tiche [the slave] had no cover, I unfolded, and as she used the foot of my bed for a pillow, gave her the other end of it, thus (tell it not in Yankeeland, for it will never be credited) actually sleeping under the same bedclothes with our black, shiny negro nurse! We are grateful, though, even for these discomforts."[78]

"The End of All Things"

As the war progressed and life grew more difficult for families in the South, practicalities became more important than patriotism. Women who had enthusiastically sent their men off to war became convinced that the fight for slavery and states' rights was not worth the sacrifice.

Southern refugees encamp in the woods near Vicksburg, Mississippi. Many Southern women were forced to flee their homes with only the few belongings they and their children could carry.

Many reluctantly admitted that they would be willing to return to the Union if they could have their husbands and fathers with them again. Georgian Julia Davidson wrote to her husband, "Oh how I do pray this war was at an end. If the Yankees are going to whip us I wish they would hurry about it."[79]

By late 1864, when it became clear that the North would likely win the conflict, women insisted that their men return to protect and aid them. Most pleaded with them directly. For instance, Octavia Stephens pointed out in a letter to her husband, "[It is foolish to] talk of the defense of your home & country for you can not defend them, they are too far gone now so give up before it is too late."[80] A few, like Margaret Easterling, wrote straight to Jefferson Davis: "I need not tell you of my devotion to my country. . . . But I want my oldest boy at home."[81]

When the end finally came, Southern women felt even more bitterness than their men did. They had seen no adventure. Their husbands, if alive, were often mentally and physically broken. Their farms and plantations were in ruins, and they no longer had a source of free help to rebuild them. With the North in control, a new order was coming to their world. There was nothing positive to look forward to, as McDonald concluded. "I felt as if the end of all things had come, at least for the Southern people. Grief and despair took possession of my heart, with a sense of humiliation that till then I did not know I could feel."[82]

Chapter Four

Cities, Sacrifice, and Survival

There were few large cities or towns in the South during the Civil War. New Orleans, Louisiana, was the largest, with a population of almost 170,000. By comparison, New York City had a population of about 800,000 at the time. The next largest Southern cities were Charleston, South Carolina; Richmond, Virginia; and Mobile, Alabama, with populations of between 29,000 and 40,500. Other significant but smaller towns included Memphis, Tennessee; Savannah, Georgia; and Petersburg, Virginia, with between 18,000 and 23,000 citizens. Atlanta, Georgia, had less than 10,000 residents. Today it boasts more than 432,000.

Despite their limited number, cities were important to the war effort. People in them worked in manufacturing businesses that made tents, uniforms, harnesses, swords, bayonets, and other war materiel. They worked on railroads, loading and unloading goods. They organized fund-raising projects and carried out vital volunteer work. In Charlottesville, Virginia, a widow named Ada Bacot expressed the feelings of many when she said, "Now I can give myself up to my state, the very thought elevates me. These long years I have prayed for something to do, perhaps my prayer is now being answered."[83]

Doing Business

The exemption clause of the Confederacy's conscription act allowed thousands of urban men to remain at their jobs during the war because they were carrying out services vital to the country. Thus, shoemakers, tanners, blacksmiths, wagon makers, and the like continued to work at their jobs, turning out everything from boots to saddles. Superintendents of factories oversaw the making of munitions; newspaper owners and reporters kept the country updated on the latest war news; and ministers provided spiritual support and encouragement to their congregations. Although jobs requiring heavy manual labor were usually filled by men and slaves, others were filled by women. The idea of women working outside the home for pay was frowned on, but patriotic or needy women overlooked the criticism and swallowed their own scruples for the cause. Lila Chunn of Georgia wrote to her husband: "It looks funny in Dixie to see a lady behind the counter. . . . The idea of a lady having to face and transact business with any and every body. It is alone suited to the North(ern) women of brazen faces. But I say if it is necessary, our ladies ought to shopkeep and do everything else they can to aid in the great struggle for Liberty."[84]

> **WORDS IN CONTEXT**
>
> **the cause**
>
> The Confederate conviction that states had the right to secede; it motivated Southerners to fight the Civil War.

Many women chose to fill teaching positions that had previously been filled by men. They were comfortable caring for children, so teaching seemed a logical next step. Women who were more daring went to work for the government, finding employment as seamstresses sewing uniforms, ordnance workers making cartridges, and clerks in the post office, commissary, or treasury department. With their elegant handwriting, women in the treasury signed hundreds of thousands of Confederate banknotes by hand, while others cut up the sheets on which the bills were printed. Upper-class women like Mary Chesnut vowed never to become so common and unrefined. "Survive or perish—we will not go into one of the departments. We will not stand up all day and cut notes apart, ordered round by a department clerk."[85]

"The Most Cheerless Place in the World"

Just as the thought of working for pay outside the home was repellent to many Southern women, caring for the wounded also offended their

Workers make gun carriages for the Confederate army in Richmond, Virginia. Men with skills essential to supporting the war effort— shoemakers, blacksmiths, makers of munitions, and others—were exempt from conscription.

notions of respectability. Married women might care for their sick husbands, give them baths, or change their clothes, but they would not think of doing the same for any other man. Nevertheless, women were regularly called on to perform nursing duties in city hospitals. Men wounded on the battlefield were usually transported there because conditions were safer and better care was available than in field hospitals. The small community of Winchester, Virginia, faced an influx of three thousand wounded soldiers after the Battle of Antietam in 1862. Ten thousand wounded men poured into the town of Lynchburg, Virginia, after the Battle of the Wilderness in May 1864. Mary Lee observed, "All that I had conceived of the horrors of battles sinks into insignificance

In Their Own Words

An Eloquent Plea

As the Confederate army ran short of supplies during the war, citizens were asked to donate anything they could to the military. The following article, originally printed on October 19, 1863, in the *Daily Mississippian* newspaper, was a plea from Captain W.M. Gillespie, who was responsible for outfitting the army in Alabama.

> I want all the blankets and carpets that can possibly be spared. I want them, ladies of Alabama, to shield your noble defenders against an enemy more to be dreaded than the Northern foe with musket in hand—the snows of coming winter. Do you know that thousands of our heroic soldiers of the West sleep on the cold, damp ground without tents? Perhaps not. You enjoy warm houses and comfortable beds. If the immortal matrons and maidens of heathen Rome could shear off and twist into bowstrings the hair of their heads to arm their husbands in repelling the invader, will not the Christian women of the Confederacy give the carpets off their floors to protect against the chilly blasts of winter those who are fighting with more than Roman heroism, for their lives, liberty, and more, their honor?

Quoted in Central Library of Rochester and Monroe County: Historic Serials Collection, Rochester (NY) Soldier's Aid, January 6, 1864. www.libraryweb.org.

compared with the sights of the day—the streets have been crowded with ambulances bringing in thousands of wounded men."[86]

Most women served as volunteers. The most sensitive maintained their modesty by just bringing in food, feeding patients, swatting flies, and writing letters home for patients. Others, however, steeled themselves to wash wounds, change bandages, and assist surgeons. All had to get used to the sight of piles of amputated arms and legs, the smell of refuse, gangrene, and unwashed bodies, as well as the loud moans of the suffering. Kate Cumming, who cared for wounded soldiers on the battlefronts, observed, "A hospital is the most cheerless place in the world, and the last place I would remain in from choice. If it were not for the sake of the wounded and sick men I do not think I could possibly stand it."[87]

Some women took on hospital jobs for pay, serving as cooks and laundresses. A few exceptional ones assumed managerial duties, organizing and directing laundry, kitchen, and nursing staffs. By 1862 a committee on hospitals had recognized the benefits of having them in such positions. When males were in charge, the report read, the death rate averaged 10 percent, but when females served as managers, it was only 5 percent. Juliet Hopkins, matron and superintendent of several hospitals in Richmond, was so appreciated that one man paid her the ultimate compliment: "If you had been a man you would have been a commanding general."[88]

Aid Societies

Although many well-to-do women hesitated to go out to work or do hospital nursing, they were still eager to serve and found ways to provide for the many needs that the Confederate government could not or did not supply. More than one thousand soldiers' aid societies were formed in Confederate cities during the war. Because of their numbers and their members' varied talents, they were usually well-organized and highly effective.

Like rural women, many volunteers spent hours cutting and sewing jackets, trousers, haversacks, and even mattresses. While they sewed, others put their efforts into knitting socks, gloves, winter scarves, and small blankets for soldiers. Some were so accomplished they could knit one complete sock every day, overwhelming soldiers with their offerings. Chesnut observed that "one poor man said he had dozens of socks and just one shirt. He preferred more shirts and fewer stockings."[89]

Because there was always a need for money to purchase supplies for the war, women in urban aid societies organized concerts or plays and sold tickets to performances. Some of the most popular forms of performance were known as *tableau vivants*, or living pictures. Even the shyest women were willing to participate if they did not have to speak, and some, like Maria Hubard of Virginia, found it thrilling to be in front of an audience. "This day will long be remembered by me, as one of the most remarkable of my life, as I made my first appearance in public,"[90] she wrote in December 1861. Aid societies raised thousands of dollars with such charitable entertainments. The funds were used for everything from supporting needy families to the creation of new hospitals and the purchase of gunboats to protect their cities.

> **WORDS IN CONTEXT**
>
> *tableau vivant*
>
> A group of posed and costumed individuals expressing a patriotic or theatrical theme.

The Verge of Starvation

No matter if urban women were upper class or poor, they all felt the pinch of war when it came to their own households. Under the Union blockade, they experienced shortages of vital goods such as clothing and medicine. And, unlike country dwellers, they did not raise their own food, so they were at the mercy of shopkeepers even for such essentials as flour, salt, sugar, and meat. As all kinds of foodstuff became harder to get and the value of Confederate money dropped, even those who could afford to pay for supplies complained of the cost. Chesnut wrote, "A thousand dollars have slipped through my fingers already this week. At the Commissary's I spent five hundred to-day for candles, sugar, and a lamp, etc."[91]

As time passed and desperation grew, poorer families found themselves wearing rags and living on the verge of starvation. Sarah Morgan Dawson wrote:

Women hang and fold laundry outside a Tennessee hospital during the Civil War. Many Southern women helped out in hospitals; their tasks ranged from washing wounds and changing bandages to washing laundry and writing letters for wounded soldiers.

For ten days, mother writes, they have lived off just hominy [hulled and treated kernels of corn] enough to keep their bodies and souls from parting, without being able to procure another article—not even a potato. Mother is not in a condition to stand such privation; day by day she grows weaker on her new regimen; I am satisfied that two months more of danger, difficulties, perplexities, and starvation will lay her in her grave.[92]

Many blamed the government for economic mismanagement, and in some cities desperate women took to the streets to protest the high prices and shortages. In April 1863 in Macon, Atlanta, and Augusta, Georgia, armed mobs attacked stores and warehouses in an effort to find food. In Salisbury, North Carolina, they broke down shop doors with hatchets and threatened storekeepers. In Richmond thousands broke into shops and began to seize clothing, shoes, food, and even jewelry. Jefferson Davis himself went out to try to pacify them. He threw them what money he had in his pockets, saying, "You say you are hungry and have no money; here, this is all I have."[93] Unsatisfied, the rioters remained and did not go home until Davis threatened to have militiamen fire on them.

Occupied by the Enemy

In addition to shortages caused by the war, some city dwellers endured occupation by the enemy for months on end. Occupations took place in New Orleans; Memphis and Nashville, Tennessee; Norfolk and Alexandria, Virginia; and other towns in the South. Alexandria was occupied the longest. It was held by federal troops from May 1861 until the end of the war.

Under occupation, residents—the majority of them women and children—were allowed to live seminormal lives. The Union was well-supplied, so food was usually available, although prices were high. Union soldiers patrolled the streets and kept crime in check. However, residents lost many of their freedoms and, in New Orleans, had to submit to taking an oath of allegiance if they wanted to stay. Military laws prohibited speaking against, writing against, or committing any act of defiance against the occupiers.

As a result, businessmen who refused to serve Yankees were imprisoned. Newspaper offices that printed stories sympathetic to the Confederacy were closed or burned. Not even ministers were exempt. When one episcopal rector in Alexandria omitted the prayer for the president of the United States, printed in the Episcopal prayer book, Union soldiers in the congregation arrested him. Joseph Blount Cheshire, then Bishop of North Carolina, recalled: "A captain and his soldiers, who were present in the congregation for the purpose, drew their swords and pistols, intruded into the chancel, seized the clergyman . . . held pistols to his head, and forced him out of the church, and through the streets, just as he was, in his surplice and stole, and committed him to the guard-house of the 8th Illinois Cavalry."[94]

Looking Back

Boarding Schools

Southern traditions held that women—especially young, unmarried women—needed to be protected from the harsh realities of life. During the war parents did all they could to safeguard their daughters, and as Drew Gilpin Faust explains in her book *Mothers of Invention*, those who could afford it sent them to boarding schools.

> The safety and purity of young white girls was a particular concern in the wartime South, for they were seen as especially vulnerable in case of enemy invasion or slave uprising. Many families exerted considerable effort to keep them away from areas of military action and upheaval. "It was thought safer for a young girl just grown up to be well out of the reach of Yankee soldiery," one South Carolina mother remarked. Boarding schools offered one solution to this difficulty. Male colleges and academies closed their doors as men left the classroom for the battlefield, but many women's schools thrived. Hollins College [in Virginia] enrolled 83 students in 1861–62 but had grown to 160 by 1864–65. J.F. Dagg, president of the Baptist Female College of Southwest Georgia, faced continual wartime disruptions . . . but the school expanded nonetheless, from 36 pupils in 1861 to 82 by 1863 to 103 [in 1864].

Drew Gilpin Faust, *Mothers of Invention*. Chapel Hill: University of North Carolina Press, 1996, p. 39.

Sneers and Sarcasm

While men showed obvious defiance, Southern women were skilled at more subtle forms of rebellion. For instance, they crossed streets to avoid walking past Union soldiers. They avoided eye contact with Yankee soldiers by wearing sunbonnet-type hats with wide projecting brims, nicknamed "Jeff Davis bonnets." They made sneering or sarcastic remarks under their breath and twitched aside their skirts when passing Union troops on the street. Historian Robert S. Holzman wrote, "One patriotic woman twirled her skirts so violently . . . that she fell in the gutter."[95]

Depending on the Union commander, such activities were usually allowed to pass unnoticed. But when Union general Benjamin Butler, head of occupying forces in New Orleans, heard of the continued snubs his men endured, he passed the so-called Women's Order. It stated that "when any female shall, by word, gesture, or movement, insult or show contempt for any officer or soldier of the United States, she shall be regarded . . . as a woman of the town [prostitute] plying her avocation."[96]

> **WORDS IN CONTEXT**
>
> **"Butlerize"**
>
> A term used by New Orleans women to describe an attack by soldiers as a result of Union general Benjamin Butler's "Women's Order."

Not surprisingly, women were outraged at the pronouncement, fearing that they would be attacked, or as they called it, "Butlerized." Some even went so far as to carry some form of protection. Dawson wrote in her diary, "Come to my bosom, O my discarded carving-knife, laid aside under the impression that these men were gentlemen. We will be close friends once more. And if you must have a sheath, perhaps I may find one for you in the heart of the first man who attempts to Butlerize me."[97]

Besieged

Although some cities were easy to capture, others were, for various reasons, more difficult for Union armies to take. Two of the most stubborn holdouts were Vicksburg, Mississippi, and Petersburg, Virginia. Vicksburg was set on a hill overlooking the Mississippi River and was

The Union army's siege of Petersburg, Virginia (pictured) beginning in 1864 brought ruin to this once prosperous and sophisticated city. Many residents fled to nearby woods and fields; others fortified their basements or built bomb shelters in their back yards.

well fortified in all directions. Petersburg was also well fortified, with multiple lines of earthworks (protective embankments) and trenches behind which Confederate defenders could repel invaders. In order to take such cities, Union generals put them under siege, a military operation in which they surrounded and bombarded them, cutting off supplies and outside help until defenders surrendered. Vicksburg was besieged in May 1863 and Petersburg in June 1864.

Inside both towns during the sieges, citizens watched their homes, neighborhoods, and lives descend into ruin. Before the war, Petersburg's eighteen thousand residents lived in a prosperous, sophisticated city with gas streetlights, brick sidewalks, two daily newspapers, a multitude of textile mills, tobacco companies, and more than 150 grocery stores. Vicksburg, a town of about five thousand people, had its share of banks, hotels, and shops, as well as neighborhoods of expensive homes overlooking the Mississippi.

Once the firing started, however, all that changed. Shells from hundreds of cannons and mortars rained down day and night, blowing holes in streets and buildings. Chimneys collapsed. Trees were blasted. Soon, few buildings remained undamaged. English traveler Edward Moseley described conditions in Petersburg: "The city presented the most desolate appearance—public buildings, warehouses, private houses . . . clearly bore evidence of the effects of the heavy shelling. . . . Not a hotel open in the place, or the slightest appearance of any business having been carried on for some time."[98]

Bomb Shelters and Caves

Many people fled cities at the beginning of a siege, but others had nowhere to go. To escape the terrifying missiles in Petersburg, residents moved to outlying woods or fields, camping there and surviving on anything they could scrape together. "What they live on their Heavenly father only knows,"[99] wrote John Claiborne, medical director of hospitals in the city. Other residents moved into their basements, which they fortified with sandbags, bales of cotton, and even mattresses. Still others dug bomb shelters, known as bombproofs, in their back yards.

In Vicksburg, residents hollowed out caves in the town's hillsides and sheltered there. These caves could be simple holes or several rooms furnished with rugs, chairs, and beds scavenged from houses. At one point more than five hundred such hideouts existed in the town. One resident wrote: "Caves were the fashion—the rage—over besieged Vicksburg. Negroes . . . hired themselves out to dig them, at from thirty to fifty dollars, according to their size. . . . So great was the demand for cave workmen, that a new branch of industry sprang up and became popular."[100]

Eventually, many residents grew accustomed to the constant shelling. A Virginia cavalryman in Petersburg remarked that "it was really refreshing to see ladies pass coolly along the streets as though nothing unusual was transpiring while the 160-pound shells were howling . . . through the smoky air and bursting in the very heart of the city, . . . even the children would stand and watch, at the sound of the passing shells, to see the explosion."[101] Others never got used to the danger. A woman in Vicksburg wrote, "People do nothing but eat what they can get, sleep when they can, and dodge the shells."[102]

Intolerable Conditions

Whether besieged city dwellers coped well with shelling or not, they suffered from being cut off from supplies. Firewood ran out, so trees, furniture, and other available pieces of wood were scavenged. The editor of the *Petersburg Express* newspaper observed in March 1865, "Nearly every little foot bridge about town has lost half of its timber while some of them have entirely disappeared."[103]

Food was especially scarce. If it could be found, it was extremely expensive. By the end of 1864, for instance, flour cost $1,300 a barrel in Petersburg. Eventually people were left with little but potatoes and cornmeal. One woman wrote, "[I am] so tired of cornbread, which I never liked, that I eat it with tears in my eyes."[104] Desperate for meat, people trapped and ate pigeons, rats, and even dogs. When one Confederate soldier gave a Vicksburg girl a jaybird for a pet, the child's mother ruthlessly made it into soup.

Inevitably, when conditions became intolerable, city leaders surrendered. Vicksburg fell to Union troops on July 4, 1863. At Petersburg, Confederate soldiers slipped out of the city at the end of March 1865, after having set fire to tobacco warehouses, bridges, and other structures so they would not fall into enemy hands. One of the last to leave, Confederate I.G. Bradwell, remembered, "As we passed the houses in the city the women peeped out and said to us sadly: 'Good-by Rebels; we never expect to see you again.'"[105]

Up in Flames

Fire was often used as a weapon in cities, if not by Confederates, then by Union troops who aimed to weaken resistance. Ten-year-old Carrie Berry, whose parents refused to evacuate after Atlanta, Georgia, was set afire by Sherman's soldiers in late 1864, wrote: "Oh what a night we had. They came burning the store house and about night it looked like the whole town was on fire. We all set up all night. If we had not set up our house would have been burnt up for the fire was very near and the soldiers were going around setting houses on fire where they were not watched. They behaved very badly."[106]

No one is sure who was responsible for the burning of Columbia, South Carolina, which went up in flames in 1865. As Sherman's forces marched in and set fire to railroad depots, arsenals, and machine shops, retreating Southerners on the other side of the city lit stores of cotton bales on fire. High winds did their part to spread burning embers. Seventeen-year-old resident Emma LeConte recorded the event in her diary: "The wind blew a fearful gale, wafting the flames from house to house with frightful rapidity. By midnight the whole town (except the outskirts) was wrapped in one huge blaze. . . . What a scene! It was about four o'clock and the State House was one grand conflagration."[107]

WORDS IN CONTEXT

arsenals

Buildings for storage of weapons and ammunition.

Whether their cities were spared or destroyed by fire, cannons, or mortar, by the end of the war, city dwellers found themselves—like rural folks—in much worse condition than they had been at the war's beginning. Repairing and rebuilding their lives would take years of work, and they had no money to take on such projects. At times they had to accept food and medicine from the hated enemy. Most bitter was the fact that their own actions had led them to such humiliation. Eliza Frances Andrews echoed the words of countrywoman Cornelia Peake McDonald when she said: "Everything is in a state of disorganization and tumult. We have no currency, no law save the primitive code that might makes right. . . . At present nobody dares to make any plans for the future. We can only wait each day for what the morrow may bring forth. Oh, we are utterly and thoroughly wretched."[108]

Chapter Five

Divided Loyalties

At the beginning of the war, more than 4 million people in the South—about one-half of the population—were slaves. Their lives were ones of drudgery and hopelessness. They were bought and sold like animals, worked long hours for no pay, and were whipped or even killed if they did not meet their owners' expectations. Most slave women did the same work as men, which included steering heavy wooden plows, hoeing, planting, picking, and toting heavy loads.

House slaves, who had easier lives than those in the fields, were still overworked and mistreated. Lewis Clarke, who did everything from rocking cradles to weeding the kitchen garden and spinning flax, recalled, "We were constantly exposed to the whims and passions of every member of the family; from the least to the greatest their anger was wreaked [inflicted] upon us. Nor was our life an easy one, in the hours of our toil or in the amount of labor performed. We were always required to sit up until all the family had retired; then we must be up at early dawn in summer, and before day in winter."[109]

During the war years, slaves suffered through the same difficult experiences that their owners did. Ex-slave Andrew Moss of Georgia said: "Talk about hard times! We see'd 'em in dem days, durin' the war. . . . We was glad to eat ash-cakes and drink parched corn and rye 'stead o' coffee. I've seed my grandmother go to de smoke house, and scrape up de dirt whar de meat had dropped, and take it to de house for seasonin.'"[110] Unlike their white owners, however, slaves were encouraged by the thought that the North might win the war. Such a win, they were convinced, would result in their freedom. Former slave Wiley Nealy remembered, "Liberty and Freedom was all I ever heard any colored folks say dey expected to get out of de war, and mighty proud of dot [that]. . . . Didn't nobody want land, they jess wanted freedom."[111]

Yearning for Freedom

To slaves there were few things more important than freedom. Although they were uneducated and ill informed, they knew that the United States had been founded on the assumption that all men were created equal and deserved the right of freedom. Their masters saw them as less than human, but they knew in their hearts that they were not and believed that they deserved to enjoy the same rights and opportunities as other Americans.

Slaves also yearned for freedom as an escape from the cruel burden of never-ending work and ill treatment they endured. Ex-slave Louis Hughes observed, "Perhaps they would not have thought of freedom, if their owners had not been so cruel. Had my mistress been more kind to me, I should have thought less of liberty. I know the cruel treatment which I received was the main thing that made me wish to be free."[112]

With freedom always on their minds, slaves realized before Northern politicians did that the Civil War was likely to be their salvation. One anonymous slave stated, "Our union friends Says the(y) are not fighting to free the negroes we are fighting for the union. . . . Very well let the white fight for what the(y) want and we negroes fight for what we want. . . . Liberty must take the day."[113] Some did not understand that being free would involve hard work and that they would be responsible for getting their own jobs, food, shelter, clothing, and so on. But all yearned to have the chance to have a say in their lives, to be able to come and go, work or rest, live or die on their own terms.

Personal Ties

Despite slaves' desire for freedom, there were many whose loyalty to the South tied them to the side of the Confederacy. It was home to them— a place where they had friends, family, and cultural ties. In addition, many slaves were suspicious of Northerners. They had been taught by their masters that Yankees were monsters or devils with horns who would

Many slaves on Southern plantations continued to work at the jobs they had been forced to do before the war. Like others left behind once the war began, the slaves experienced hunger and fear, but many also held out hope of freedom.

hang them, drown them, or send them to a foreign country if given the chance. Ex-slave Richard Franklin recalled, "I thought the Yankees would kill me, because my master told me that the Yankees were bad people."[114]

It was not uncommon for black slaves to feel strong ties to their white family; this was the only family some of the slaves had ever known. Hundreds of loyal male body servants accompanied well-to-do Southern men when they went off to war. At times a unit of two thousand white soldiers would have as many as one thousand male slaves attached to it. Such slaves cooked, cleaned, and waited on their masters as they had at home. The slaves took care of the horses, foraged for food, nursed sick or wounded masters, and escorted their bodies back home in the event of death.

Many of these slaves not only acted as servants, they insisted on going into battle with their masters and did not hesitate to kill Yankees

69

In Their Own Words

"Free Right Now"

The Emancipation Proclamation motivated many slaves to seek freedom in 1863. Boston Blackwell, enslaved in Georgia and Arkansas, was one such man, and he recounts his experience in an interview with a member of the Federal Writers' Project in 1937.

You know Abraham Lincoln 'claired freedom in '63, first day of January. In October '63, I runned away and went to Pine Bluff [Arkansas] to get to the Yankees. . . . The young boy what cut the whips, he named Jerry, he come along wif me, and we wade the stream for a long piece. Then we hide in dark woods. It was cold, frosty weather. Two days and two nights we traveled. That boy, he so cold and hungry he want to fall out by the way, but I drug him on.

When we gets to the Yankee camp all our troubles was over. We gets all the contraband [food taken by Union troops] we could eat. Was they more runaways there? Oh, Lordy, yessum. Hundreds, I reckon. Yes-sum, the Yankees feeds all them refugees on contraband. They made me a driver of a team in the quarter-master's department. I was always keerful to do everything they told me. They telled me I was free when I gets to the Yankee camp, but I couldn't go outside much. Yessum, iffen you could get to the Yankees' camp you was free right now.

Quoted in National Humanities Center, "The Making of African American Identity, Vol. 1, 1500–1865," 2009. http://nationalhumanitiescenter.org.

if they got the opportunity. A newspaper correspondent from the *New Orleans Daily Crescent* reported that during one of the early battles of the war, a servant named Levin Graham refused to stay in camp during a battle, "but obtained a musket, fought manfully, and killed four of the Yankees himself."[115] There were also instances when black servants were captured along with their masters and chose to share the hardship of prison rather than going free.

Protectors

While body servants were loyal in the field, other slaves remained on plantations and farms and worked virtually unsupervised, sharing their white family's efforts to survive the war. Any suggestion that they would be better off if they ran away was met with a refusal. Sarah Morgan Dawson told of her mother's slave, Margret, who said, "I don't want to be any free-er than I is now—I'll stay with my mistress."[116]

Such loyal slaves often took on even greater responsibilities than they had had before the war, feeling that it was their job to help protect their white mistresses and children when the master was away. Cato Carter of Alabama was one such servant. He recalled: "When massa and the other mens on the place went off to war, he called me and said, 'Cato, you's allus been a 'sponsible man, and I leave you to look after the women

> **WORDS IN CONTEXT**
> **ash-cake**
> Cornbread baked in hot ashes.

and the place. If I don't come back, I want you to allus stay by Missie Adeline!' I said, ''Fore Gawd, I will, Massa Oll.'"[117]

On many occasions, slaves hid the family's valuables in their own cabins to protect them from the enemy and stood willing to defend the family when Northern troops arrived. Ex-slave Rivana Boynton and other house slaves begged Union soldiers to spare their mistress's life when she would not reveal where her silver was hidden. Boynton recalled, "They took potatoes and all the hams they wanted, but they left our Missus 'cause we save her life."[118]

Rebelling and Running Away

Although there were slaves who were loyal to their white families, there were many others who felt that their own freedom and welfare came first. Thus, when they saw that they were no longer as carefully controlled as they had been before, they began to rebel against those who were, in essence, their enemies. They worked more slowly, disobeyed orders, stole food, and left the plantation to visit friends without permission. When enemy troops arrived, they pointed out where the valuables were hidden. Former slave Samuel Bouleware of South Carolina explained: "I 'members lak yesterday, de Yankees comin' 'long. Marster tried to hide the best stuff on de plantation but some of de slaves dat helped him hide it, showed de Yankee soldiers just where it was, when they come dere. . . . Then de soldiers went straight to de place where de valuables was hid and dug them out and took them."[119]

Many slaves took advantage of lax supervision and ran away. Early in the war, only the bravest men—those who lived in border states and close to Union lines—dared to do so, but as time passed, more men, women, and children decided to take the risk. Often they slipped away at night, when supervision was lightest. In Middleburg, Virginia, slave owner Catherine Cochran recalled, "scarcely a morning dawned that some stampede was not announced—sometimes persons would awake to find every servant gone & we never went to bed without anticipating such an occurrence."[120] Freedom tempted even those who seemed to be in comfortable, prestigious positions. For instance, Mary Chesnut wrote: "The President's man, Jim, that he believed in as we all believe in our own servants, 'our own people,' as we call them, and Betsy, Mrs. Davis's maid, decamped [left] last night. . . . At Mrs. Davis's the hired servants all have been birds of passage."[121]

Seeking Protection

Before the war, runaway slaves had to travel hundreds of miles to get to the safety of a free state, but with the coming of Union troops into the South, safety was often just a few miles away. Thousands of slaves fled to Union encampments, where commanders protected them from recap-

A slave couple and their child escape on horseback in the night. Some slaves took advantage of the chaos and distractions of war to escape to the North.

ture. "(The slaves followed the army) like a sable cloud in the sky before a thunderstorm," declared a Union officer. "They thought it was freedom now or never."[122]

Northerners had not planned for such a flood of runaways and often struggled to care for them. They settled some on abandoned plantations, but most were placed in camps, where they were given tents, rations, and sometimes pay in exchange for cleaning, digging trenches, building fortifications, and the like. The camps were far from perfect refuges, however.

All were crowded and chaotic. Runaways were often sick and starving, and living in tents did not help their condition. Hundreds of women and children died for lack of care. A Union commander in Tennessee wrote, "The suffering from hunger and cold is so great that those wretched people are dying by scores . . . sometimes 30 per day die and are carried out by wagon loads, without coffins, and thrown promiscuously, like brutes, into a trench."[123] Many slaves also suffered abuse at the hands of Union guards who resented having to "play nursemaid" and took advantage of their ignorance and powerlessness. A *New York Evening Post* war correspondent reported, "Many, very many of the soldiers and not a few of the officers have habitually treated the negroes with the coarsest and most brutal insolence and humanity; never speaking to them but to curse and revile them."[124]

> **WORDS IN CONTEXT**
>
> sable cloud
>
> A black storm cloud.

On the other hand, in some camps commanders appointed superintendents to oversee refugees' welfare. Often private relief associations like the American Missionary Society stepped in to provide supplies, supervision, and education. In this setting, slaves had a chance to experience freedom for the first time. A Union provost marshal (head of military police) in Louisiana wrote, "They have obtained in the camps . . . a spirit of independence—a feeling that they are no longer slaves."[125]

Inside Information

Although black runaways were a burden on the Union army, they also proved valuable as informers because they had detailed information about conditions in areas from which they had fled. Robert E. Lee stated in May 1863, "The chief source of information to the enemy is through our negroes."[126] With their inside knowledge, slave informants could direct Union foragers to unprotected plantations where supplies and valuables were hidden. Personal servants whose owners talked freely in front of them could report on Confederate military plans. For instance, three officers' servants who escaped from a Confederate camp outside Charleston, South Carolina, in 1863 were able

Looking Back

Slave Women

White women were not the only females who struggled against adversity during the Civil War. Slave women carried extra burdens because they could be abused and then abandoned, as the article "Women in the Civil War" explains.

> Slave women were, of course, not free to contribute to the Union cause. Moreover, they had never had the luxury of "true womanhood" to begin with. As one historian pointed out, "being a woman never saved a single female slave from hard labor, beatings, rape, family separation, and death." The Civil War promised freedom, but it also added to these women's burden. In addition to their own plantation and household labor, many slave women had to do the work of their husbands and partners too: The Confederate Army frequently impressed [forced into military service] male slaves, and slaveowners fleeing from Union troops often took their valuable male slaves, but not women and children, with them.

History.com, "Women in the Civil War," 2013. www.history.com.

to give the Union information on the condition of Fort Sumter that helped with its recapture in 1865.

In another instance of a slave supplying vital war intelligence, a woman named Marie Louvestre provided the North with information on the South's progress in creating the first ironclad vessel, the *Merrimac*. Both sides in the war were eager to create ironclad ships in order to have the advantage in naval battles. Louvestre served a Confederate engineer who was working on the *Merrimac*, and she stole paperwork and carried it to US secretary of the navy Gideon Welles. Welles reported, "[Louvestre] told me the condition of the vessel, and took from her clothing a paper, written by a mechanic who was working on the *Merrimac*, describing the character of the work, its progress and probable completion."[127]

Thanks to Louvestre, the Union navy intensified construction of its own ironclad, the *Monitor*, and sailed it down to Virginia, where it engaged the *Merrimac* in the world's first ironclad naval battle. The battle effectively kept the Confederate navy from breaking the federal blockade that had cut off Virginia's largest cities, Norfolk and Richmond, from international trade.

WORDS IN CONTEXT

insolence

Insulting; showing contempt in speech or conduct.

Emancipation

Whether they served as informants or remained on plantations, when slaves heard the news of the signing of the Emancipation Proclamation on January 1, 1863, their dreams of freedom were suddenly realized. Ironically, many did not learn about emancipation until long afterward. Fanny Griffin, enslaved in South Carolina, recalled, "We ain't know we was free 'til a good while after. We ain't know it 'til [Confederate] General [Joseph] Wheeler come thru and tell us. After that, de massa and missus let all de slaves go 'cepting me; they kept me to work in de house and de garden."[128] Slaveholders in Galveston, Texas, managed to keep the news from their slaves until June 19, 1865, when Union soldiers arrived and informed them they were free.

When given their freedom, slaves reacted in different ways. Some danced and celebrated for days. Some were quietly grateful. Future author, orator, and political leader Booker T. Washington recalled that his family's emancipation day arrived when the war ended. He recalled:

Some man who seemed to be a stranger (a United States officer, I presume) made a little speech and then read a rather long paper—the Emancipation Proclamation, I think. After the reading we were told that we were all free, and could go when and where we pleased. My mother, who was standing by my side, leaned over and kissed her children, while tears of joy ran down her cheeks. She explained to us what it all meant, that this was the day for which she had been so long praying, but fearing that she would never live to see.[129]

Some two hundred thousand slaves chose to leave their homes upon hearing they were emancipated. One woman remembered, "Was wintertime and mighty cold that night, but everybody commenced getting ready to leave. Didn't care nothin' about Missus."[130]

A messenger brings news of the Emancipation Proclamation to Southern slaves. Reactions differed, with some slaves celebrating for days and others quietly pondering their future.

The Ultimate Outcome

Totally inexperienced, many of these runaways had no plans for where they were going or what they would do when they got there. Henry Bobbitt of North Carolina recalled, "De first year I slept in folkses wood-houses an' barns an' in de woods or any whar else I could find. I wucked hyar an' dar [worked here and there], but de folkses' jist give me sompin' ter eat an' my clothes wuz in strings 'fore de spring o' de year."[131] Like Bobbitt, many lived a hand-to-mouth existence, while others returned to their former homes when they became too hungry and discouraged.

Some of the newly freed slaves were wise enough to foresee such difficulties. They remained with their former owners, who now had to pay them for their work. Daniel Waring of South Carolina recalled, "We didn't know where to go or what to do, and so we stayed right where we was, . . . I 'member my mammy tellin' me that food was gittin' scarce, and any black folks beginnin' to scratch for themselves would suffer, if they take their foot in their hand and ramble 'bout the land."[132]

Whether slaves left or stayed, emancipation marked the end of what former slave Frederick Douglass termed "devilish outrages"[133] against an entire race of people. And by the war's end, everyone realized that the slaves had been right—the struggle had really been all about their freedom. Historian Barbara Fields observed, "Only gradually and at great cost did the nation at large learn that the slaves were more than property . . . they were people . . . whose point of view must therefore be taken into account."[134]

A Hard Lesson

That lesson was a hard one for white Southerners to accept. And by war's end, most realized that the cost of secession had been too high. Their slaves were gone. Over a quarter million men had died of wounds and disease. About $1 billion (in 1860 dollars) had been spent and lost in the war effort. There had been at least $1.5 billion in property damage that included burned and plundered homes, lost crops and farm animals, and ruined cities and transportation systems. The destruction was almost intolerable. Eliza Frances Andrews wrote, "A settled gloom, deep and heavy, hangs over the whole land. All hearts are in mourning for the fall of our country, and all minds rebellious against the wrongs and oppression to which our cruel conquerors subject us. . . . We are overwhelmed, overpowered, and trodden underfoot . . . 'immortal hate and . . . revenge' lives in the soul of every man."[135]

That hatred and desire for revenge shaped the lives of Southerners for generations and caused them to resist the changes that were forced on them after the war. Over time, however, most adjusted to the realities of the postwar world. They grew resigned to being a part of the United States again. Their bitterness over their defeat faded, although for some, it would never be entirely forgotten.

Today in the South, the Civil War is remembered as a difficult and divisive experience. Other than putting an end to slavery, nothing good came from Southerners' insistence on fighting for the cause they believed in. If their sacrifices were in vain, though, Confederates are remembered for their courage and patriotism during a momentous time in American history.

Historian William C. Davis points out: "Living and dead, soldier and civilian, they had participated in something that set America apart, that renewed [the] nation and set it on the path to world power. In the process, they had spent their blood and their youth and experienced the greatest adventure of their generation and left their mark upon the defining moment of their century."[136]

Source Notes

Introduction: A Terrible Thing

1. Quoted in Rachel Neuwirth, "The Hard Hand of War," *American Thinker*, June 7, 2007. www.americanthinker.com.
2. Henry Hitchcock, *Marching with Sherman: Passages from the Letters and Campaign Diaries of Henry Hitchcock, Assistant Adjutant General of Volunteers, November 1864–May 1865*. Lincoln: University of Nebraska Press, 1995, p. 125.
3. Alexander H. Stephens, "Cornerstone Speech," Teaching American History.org, March 21, 1861. http://teachingamericanhistory.org.
4. Mary Boykin Miller Chesnut, *A Diary from Dixie as Written by Mary Boykin Chesnut, Wife of James Chesnut, Jr., United States Senator from South Carolina, 1859–1861, and Afterward an Aide to Jefferson Davis and a Brigadier-General in the Confederate Army*. New York: Appleton, 1905, p. 140.
5. Quoted in Geoffrey C. Ward, Ric Burns, and Ken Burns, *The Civil War: An Illustrated History*. New York: Knopf, 1990, p. 272.
6. Quoted in Eugene D. Genovese, *A Consuming Fire: The Fall of the Confederacy in the Mind of the White Christian South*. Athens: University of Georgia Press, 1998, p. 46.

Chapter One: The Burden of Leadership

7. Quoted in Ford Risley, "The South's Capital Dilemma," *Opinionator* (blog), *New York Times*, March 21, 2011. http://opinionator.blogs.nytimes.com.
8. Virginia Clay-Clopton, *A Belle of the Fifties: Memoirs of Mrs. Clay, of Alabama, Covering Social and Political Life in Washington and the South, 1853–66*. New York: Doubleday, Page, 1905, p. 173.

9. Quoted in Virginia Historical Society, "Richmond in the Midst of the Civil War," 2013. www.vahistorical.org.

10. Clay-Clopton, *A Belle of the Fifties*, p. 173.

11. Quoted in Ward et al., *The Civil War*, p. 30.

12. Quoted in Ward et al., *The Civil War*, p. 271.

13. Quoted in John Hoyt Williams, *Sam Houston: Life and Times of the Liberator of Texas, an Authentic American Hero*. New York: Touchstone, 1993, p. 252.

14. Quoted in William J. Cooper Jr., *Jefferson Davis, American*. New York: Knopf, 2000, p. 361.

15. Quoted in Bill Carey, "Old Central Built by Former Governor Who Slugged Jefferson Davis," *Vanderbilt Register*, April 8–14, 2002. www.vanderbilt.edu.

16. Quoted in Ward et al., *The Civil War*, p. 196.

17. Quoted in Ward et al., *The Civil War*, p. 195.

18. Cooper, *Jefferson Davis, American*, p. 351.

19. Quoted in Paul D. Escott, *After Secession: Jefferson Davis and the Failure of Confederate Nationalism*. Baton Rouge: Louisiana State University Press, 1978, p. 123.

20. Quoted in North Carolina Digital History, "The *Raleigh Standard* Protests Conscription," January 22, 1864. www.learnnc.org.

21. Sam R. Watkins, *"Co. Aytch," Maury Grays, First Tennessee Regiment; or, A Side Show of the Big Show*. Dayton, OH: Morningside Bookshop, 1982, p. 4.

22. Quoted in Robert F. Durden, *The Gray and the Black; The Confederate Debate on Emancipation*. Baton Rouge: Louisiana State University Press, 1972, p. 59.

23. Quoted in Durden, *The Gray and the Black*, p. 64.

24. Quoted in Ward et al., *The Civil War*, p. 253.

25. Quoted in Durden, *The Gray and the Black*, p. 81.

26. Quoted in Cooper, *Jefferson Davis, American*, p. 519.

27. Quoted in Grady McWhiney, "Jefferson Davis: Our Greatest Hero," American Studies at the University of Virginia, June 3, 1995. http://xroads.virginia.edu.

Chapter Two: "This Is Soldiering"

28. Watkins, *"Co. Aytch," Maury Grays, First Tennessee Regiment*, p. 13.

29. Bell Irvin Wiley, *The Life of Johnny Reb: The Common Soldier of the Confederacy*. New York: Bobbs-Merrill, 1943, pp. 288–289.

30. Wiley, *The Life of Johnny Reb*, p. 25.

31. Watkins, *"Co. Aytch," Maury Grays, First Tennessee Regiment*, p. 16.

32. Watkins, *"Co. Aytch," Maury Grays, First Tennessee Regiment*, pp. 19–20.

33. Quoted in Wiley, *The Life of Johnny Reb*, p. 30.

34. Watkins, *"Co. Aytch," Maury Grays, First Tennessee Regiment*, p. 32.

35. Quoted in Wiley, *The Life of Johnny Reb*, p. 33.

36. Watkins, *"Co. Aytch," Maury Grays, First Tennessee Regiment*, p. 189.

37. Quoted in Wiley, *The Life of Johnny Reb*, p. 35.

38. Quoted in Wiley, *The Life of Johnny Reb*, p. 307.

39. Quoted in Wiley, *The Life of Johnny Reb*, p. 247.

40. Quoted in Wiley, *The Life of Johnny Reb*, p. 98.

41. Quoted in Wiley, *The Life of Johnny Reb*, p. 134.

42. Quoted in Wiley, *The Life of Johnny Reb*, p. 198.

43. Quoted in Wiley, *The Life of Johnny Reb*, p. 42.

44. Quoted in Wiley, *The Life of Johnny Reb*, p. 244.

45. Quoted in Wiley, *The Life of Johnny Reb*, p. 249.

46. Eliza Frances Andrews, *The War-Time Journal of a Georgia Girl, 1864–1865*. New York: D. Appleton, 1908, p. 184.

47. Watkins, *"Co. Aytch," Maury Grays, First Tennessee Regiment*, p. 38.

48. Gilder Lehman Institute of American History, "Mary Epperly of Floyd County, Va., to Her Husband, Christian M. Epperly, a Confederate Private in the 54th Virginia Artillery," August 21, 1863. www.gilderlehrman.org.

49. Quoted in Wiley, *The Life of Johnny Reb*, p. 137.

50. Watkins, *"Co. Aytch," Maury Grays, First Tennessee Regiment*, p. 158.

51. Watkins, *"Co. Aytch," Maury Grays, First Tennessee Regiment*, p. 216.

Chapter Three: Isolated and Afraid

52. Quoted in Drew Gilpin Faust, *Mothers of Invention; Women of the Slaveholding South in the American Civil War*. Chapel Hill: University of North Carolina Press, 1996, p. 31.

53. Quoted in Faust, *Mothers of Invention*, p. 249.

54. Quoted in Tiffany K. Wayne, *Women's Roles in Nineteenth-Century America*. Westport, CT: Greenwood, 2007, p. 137.

55. Quoted in Faust, *Mothers of Invention*, p. 14.

56. Quoted in Faust, *Mothers of Invention*, p. 18.

57. Quoted in Faust, *Mothers of Invention*, pp. 24–25.

58. Quoted in Wiley, *The Life of Johnny Reb*, p. 100.

59. Quoted in Faust, *Mothers of Invention*, p. 49.

60. *Godey's Lady's Book*, "Dress Under Difficulties: American Civil War Fashions in the South During the Blockade," Ladies Treasury of Costume and Fashion. www.tudorlinks.com.

61. Quoted in Faust, *Mothers of Invention*, p. 129.

62. Quoted in Faust, *Mothers of Invention*, p. 57.

63. Quoted in Faust, *Mothers of Invention*, p. 64.

64. Quoted in Faust, *Mothers of Invention*, p. 59.

65. Quoted in Leon F. Litwack, *Been in the Storm So Long; The Aftermath of Slavery*. New York: Knopf, 1979, p. 60.

66. Quoted in Faust, *Mothers of Invention*, p. 59.

67. Quoted in Michael K. Honey, "The War Within the Confederacy: White Unionist of North Carolina," North Carolina Union Volunteers Project, Summer 1986. http://homepages.rootsweb.ancestry.com.

68. Cornelia Peake McDonald, *A Woman's Civil War: A Diary, with Reminiscences of the War, from March 1862*. Madison: University of Wisconsin Press, 1992, p. 104.

69. Dolly Lunt Burge, *A Woman's Wartime Journal: An Account of the Passage over Georgia's Plantation of Sherman's Army on the March to the Sea, as Recorded in the Diary by Dolly Sumner Lunt (Mrs. Thomas Burge)*. New York: Century, 1918, p. 22.

70. Burge, *A Woman's Wartime Journal*, p. 22.

71. Quoted in Faust, *Mothers of Invention*, p. 198.

72. Quoted in Faust, *Mothers of Invention*, p. 198.

73. McDonald, *A Woman's Civil War*, p. 35.

74. McDonald, *A Woman's Civil War*, p. 158.

75. Quoted in Martha Bankson Lyle, "Sarah Rodgers Rousseau Espy Diary, 1859–1868." http://home.mchsi.com.

76. McDonald, *A Woman's Civil War*, p. 166.

77. Andrews, *The War-Time Journal of a Georgia Girl, 1864–1865*, p. 162.

78. Sarah Morgan Dawson, *A Confederate Girl's Diary*. New York: Houghton Mifflin, 1913, p. 376.

79. Quoted in Faust, *Mothers of Invention*, p. 238.

80. Quoted in Faust, *Mothers of Invention*, p. 241.

81. Quoted in Faust, *Mothers of Invention*, p. 241.

82. McDonald, *A Woman's Civil War*, p. 232.

Chapter Four: Cities, Sacrifice, and Survival

83. Quoted in Faust, *Mothers of Invention*, p. 22.

84. Quoted in Faust, *Mothers of Invention*, p. 81.

85. Quoted in Faust, *Mothers of Invention*, p. 91.

86. Quoted in Jonathan M. Berkey, "A Separate Sovereignty: The Shenandoah Valley's Confederate Women," Shenandoah at War, 2011. www.shenandoahatwar.org.

87. Kate Cumming, *A Journal of Hospital Life in the Confederate Army of Tennessee from the Battle of Shiloh to the End of the War*. Louisville, KY: Morton, 1866, p. 60.

88. Quoted in Faust, *Mothers of Invention*, p. 94.

89. Quoted in Ward et al., *The Civil War*, p. 148.

90. Quoted in Faust, *Mothers of Invention*, p. 27.

91. Chesnut, *A Diary from Dixie as Written by Mary Boykin Chesnut*, p. 333.

92. Dawson, *A Confederate Girl's Diary*, pp. 342–43.

93. Quoted in Mark Wineka, "Bread Riot Revisited: Saturday Reenactment Marks 150th Anniversary of Women's Raids on Salisbury Merchants," *Salisbury (NC) Post*, March 14, 2013. www.salisburypost.com.

94. Joseph Blount Cheshire, "The Church in the Confederate States: A History of the Protestant Episcopal Church in the Confederate States," Project Canterbury. http://anglicanhistory.org.

95. Robert S. Holzman, *Stormy Ben Butler*. New York: Macmillan, 1954, p. 84.

96. Quoted in Dick Nolan, *Benjamin Franklin Butler, the Damnedest Yankee*. Novato, CA: Presidio, 1991, p. 177.

97. Dawson, *A Confederate Girl's Diary*, p. 36.

98. Quoted in Heidi Campbell-Shoaf, "Siege of Petersburg: The City and Citizens Were Impacted from the Start," HistoryNet, June 12, 2006. www.historynet.com.

99. Quoted in Noah Andre Trudeau, *The Last Citadel: Petersburg, Virginia, June 1864–April 1865*. Baton Rouge: Louisiana State University Press, 1993, p. 92.

100. Quoted in A.A. Hoehling, *Vicksburg: 47 Days of Siege*. Englewood Cliffs, NJ: Prentice-Hall, 1969, p. 134.

101. Quoted in Trudeau, *The Last Citadel*, p. 92.

102. Quoted in Ward et al., *The Civil War*, p. 238.

103. Quoted in Trudeau, *The Last Citadel*, p. 258.

104. Quoted in Hoehling, *Vicksburg*, p. 74.

105. Quoted in Trudeau, *The Last Citadel*, p. 403.

106. Quoted in American Civil War.com, "Carrie Berry Diary, August 1, 1864–January 4, 1865," 2012. http://americancivilwar.com.

107. Emma LeConte, *A Journal, Kept by Emma Florence LeConte, from Dec. 31, 1864 to Aug. 6, 1865, Written in Her Seventeenth Year and Containing a Detailed Account of the Burning of Columbia, by One Who Was an Eyewitness*. Washington DC: Historical Records Survey of the Works Progress Administration, 1938, p. 31.

108. Andrews, *The War-Time Journal of a Georgia Girl, 1864–1865*, pp. 198, 268.

Chapter Five: Divided Loyalties

109. Quoted in Spartacus Educational, "House Slaves," 2013. www.spartacus.schoolnet.co.uk.

110. Quoted in National Humanities Center, "I 'Member Well When the War was On," 2007. http://nationalhumanitiescenter.org.

111. Quoted in National Humanities Center, "Born in Slavery: Slave Narratives from the Federal Writers' Project." http://nationalhumanities center.org.

112. Louis Hughes, *Thirty Years a Slave: From Bondage to Freedom; The Institution of Slavery as Seen on the Plantation and in the Home of the Planter.* Milwaukee: South Side Printing, 1897, p. 79.

113. Quoted in Ward et al., *The Civil War*, p. 178.

114. Quoted in Herbert C. Covey and Dwight Eisnach, *What the Slaves Ate: Recollections of African American Foods and Foodways from the Slave Narratives.* Santa Barbara, CA: ABC-CLIO, 2009, p. 205.

115. Quoted in Tim Westphal, "Black Confederate Participation," Stonewall Brigade, 2009. www.stonewallbrigade.com.

116. Quoted in Dawson, *A Confederate Girl's Diary*, p. 211.

117. Quoted in National Humanities Center, "Born in Slavery."

118. Quoted in National Humanities Center, "Born in Slavery."

119. Quoted in National Humanities Center, "Born in Slavery."

120. Quoted in Faust, *Mothers of Invention*, pp. 75–76.

121. Chesnut, *A Diary from Dixie as Written by Mary Boykin Chesnut*, p. 275.

122. Quoted in Ward et al., *The Civil War*, p. 348.

123. Quoted in Eric Wills, "The Contraband of America and the Road to Freedom," *Preservation*, May/June 2011. www.preservationna tion.org.

124. Quoted in War for States' Rights, "Contraband Camps, 'Refugees Treated with Contempt,'" 2013. http://civilwar.bluegrass.net.

125. Quoted in Wills, "The Contraband of America and the Road to Freedom."

126. Quoted in *Mail Online (UK)*, "The 'Slaves' Who Were Spies: How Black Men and Women Risked Their Lives by Going Undercover During the Civil War," June 20, 2011. www.dailymail.co.uk.

127. Quoted in *Mail Online*, "The 'Slaves' Who Were Spies."

128. Quoted in National Humanities Center, "Born in Slavery."

129. Quoted in My Growth Plan.org, "Booker T. Washington," 2011. www.mygrowthplan.org.

130. Quoted in Ward et al., *The Civil War*, p. 177.

131. Quoted in National Humanities Center, "Born in Slavery."

132. Quoted in National Humanities Center, "Born in Slavery."

133. Frederick Douglass, "If There Is No Struggle, There Is No Progress," Black Past.org. www.blackpast.org.

134. Quoted in Ward et al., *The Civil War*, p. 179.

135. Andrews, *The War-Time Journal of a Georgia Girl, 1864–1865*, p. 254.

136. William C. Davis, "A Concise History of the Civil War," National Park Service, 2007. www.nps.gov.

For Further Research

Books

William J. Cooper Jr., *Jefferson Davis and the Civil War Era*. Baton Rouge: Louisiana State University Press, 2013.

Zachary Kent, *The Civil War: From Fort Sumter to Appomattox*. Berkeley Heights, NJ: Enslow, 2012.

Debra Smith, *Young Heroes of the Confederacy*. Gretna, LA: Pelican, 2012.

Christy Steele, ed., *Confederate Girl: The Diary of Carrie Berry, 1864*. Mankato, MN: Blue Earth, 2000.

Andrea Warren, *Under Siege! Three Children at the Civil War Battle for Vicksburg*. New York: Farrar, Straus and Giroux, 2009.

Internet Sources

Godey's Lady's Book, "Dress Under Difficulties: American Civil War Fashions in the South During the Blockade," Ladies Treasury of Costume and Fashion. www.tudorlinks.com/treasury/articles/acwdifficulties .html.

North Carolina Museum of History, "North Carolina and the Civil War: The Home Front," 2005. www.ncmuseumofhistory.org/exhibits/civil war/about_section4a.html.

Websites

Civil War (www.civilwar.com). Offers an overview of the war, a timeline, and information on battles, weapons, slavery, people, and more.

Civil War, National Park Service (www.nps.gov/civilwar). Covers such topics as civilian experiences, women in the war, Southern spies, religious figures, and others.

Civil War Richmond (www.mdgorman.com). Includes maps, written accounts, period photos, and information about the Confederate capital during the Civil War.

Museum of the Confederacy (www.moc.org). Offers an online collection of Confederate artifacts and information on topics such as clothing, flags, weapons, medical equipment, and more.

Shotgun's Home of the American Civil War (www.civilwarhome.com). Includes information on Civil War battles, medicine, leaders, and armies, as well as essays, articles, letters, and diaries pertaining to the period.

Index

Southern opinion about, 10
treatment of and by women, 46–49, 62
Upson Pilot (newspaper), 13
US Constitution, secession in, 12

Vance, Zebulon, 19
Vicksburg, Mississippi
population of, 63
siege of, 62–64, 65

Waring, Daniel, 78
War-Time Journal of a Georgia Girl, 1864-1865, The (Andrews, Eliza Frances), 16
Washington, Booker T., 76–77
Watkins, Sam R.
on being in battle, 30
on conditions in hospitals, 30, 32
on conscription, 23, 36
on constant marching, 29
on desertion, 37
on fighting to the end, 38
on glory of war, 26
on missing first Battle of Manassas, 29
weapons, 27
Welles, Gideon, 76
Wiley, Bell Irwin, 27, 28

Wise, John S., 25
women, 39
in besieged cities, 64–65
diaries kept by, 16, 45
fears of
Confederate soldiers, 44–45
Union soldiers, 46–48
violent slaves, 41, 44
isolation of, 39–40, 41
patriotism of, 40, 49, 53
on plantations, 41, 42–44, 46–49
as refugees, 50–51, **51**
slave, 67, **69**, 75–76
support for soldiers by
aid societies, 57–58
care packages, 40–42
hospital work by, 54–55, 57, **59**
traditional Southern role of, 39–40
treatment of Union soldiers by, 48–49, 62
workers outside of home, 34, 54, 57
"Women in the Civil War," 75
Women's Order, 62

Yancey, William L., 15
Yankees. *See* Union army/Yankees

Picture Credits

Cover: © Louie Psihoyos/Science Faction/Corbis

Art Resource, NY: 69

© Bettmann/Corbis: 14, 19, 59

© Corbis: 28, 35

A. Guillotte: 10

© Schenectady Museum; Hall of Electrical History Foundation/Corbis: 23

Thinkstock Images: 6, 7

Slaves picking cotton on a southern plantation (coloured engraving), American School, (19th century)/Private Collection/Peter Newark American Pictures/ The Bridgeman Art Library: 43

Fredericksburg family in a war torn house (oil on board), American School, (19th century)/Gettysburg National Military Park Museum, Pennsylvania, USA/Photo © Civil War Archive/The Bridgeman Art Library: 46

Southern refugees encamped in the woods near Vicksburg, from 'The Illustrated London News', 29th August 1863 (engraving), Vizetelly, Frank (1830-83)/ Private Collection/Peter Newark Military Pictures/The Bridgeman Art Library: 51

Making Confederate gun carriages at the Tredegar Iron Works at Richmond, Virginia (coloured engraving), American School, (19th century)/Private Collection/Peter Newark Military Pictures/ The Bridgeman Art Library: 55

The Fall of Petersburg to the Union Army, 2nd April 1965, engraved by Kurz & Allison, 1893 (colour litho), American School, (19th century)/Private Collection/Peter Newark American Pictures/The Bridgeman Art Library: 63

A Ride for Liberty (oil on board), Johnson, Eastman (1824-1906)/Brooklyn Museum of Art, New York, USA / Gift of Gwendolyn O.L. Conkling/The Bridgeman Art Library: 73

The Hour of Emancipation, 1863 (oil on canvas), Carlton, William Tolman (1816-1888)/Private Collection/Photo © Christie's Images/The Bridgeman Art Library: 77

About the Author

Diane Yancey is a freelance author who lives in the Pacific Northwest. She has published more than forty books, including five on the Civil War: *Civil War Generals of the Union, Leaders and Generals of the North and South, Strategic Battles of the Civil War, Frederick Douglass*, and *The Abolition of Slavery*.